Transforming Evangelism

D0020777

TRANSFORMATIONS
THE EPISCOPAL CHURCH IN THE 21ST CENTURY

Transforming Evangelism

DAVID GORTNER

CHURCH PUBLISHING
an imprint of Church Publishing Incorporated, New York

To Cassie and Miriam, and for the future of their faith

Unless otherwise indicated, all passages from the scriptures are from the *New Revised Standard Version* of the Bible. © 1989 by the Division of Christian Education of the National Council of Churches of Christ in the U.S.A. Used by permission. All rights reserved.

Library of Congress Cataloging-in-Publication Data
Gortner, David.
   Transforming evangelism / by David Gortner.
       p.   cm.
   ISBN 978-0-89869-585-4 (pbk.)
   1. Evangelistic work. I. Title.
   BV3790.G733 2008
   266'.373--dc22
                                        2007051306

Cover design by Stefan Killen Design.
Study guide and interior design by Vicki K. Black.

Printed in the United States of America.

Church Publishing, Incorporated
445 Fifth Avenue
New York, New York 10016
www.churchpublishing.com

       5   4   3   2   1

Contents

Series Preface vii

Acknowledgments ix

1. "Go Therefore and Make Disciples" 1

2. "The Road to Jerusalem is in the Heart" 33

3. Living the Pilgrim Faith:
Models of Evangelism 70

4. With Open and Courageous Hearts:
Tools for Evangelism 122

5. "Were Not Our Hearts Burning
Within Us?" 165

A Guide for Discussion 171

Resources 177

Notes and Sources 179

a note from the publisher

This series emerged as a partnership between the Office of Mission of the Episcopal Church and Church Publishing, as a contribution to the mission of the church in a new century. We would like to thank James Lemler, series editor, for bringing the initial idea to us and for facilitating the series. We also want to express our gratitude to the Office of Mission for two partnership grants: the first brought all the series authors together for two creative days of brainstorming and fellowship; and the second is helping to further publicize the books of the series to the clergy and lay people of the Episcopal Church.

Series Preface

B e ye transformed" (KJV). "Be transformed by the renewing of your minds" (NRSV). "Fix your attention on God. You'll be changed from the inside out" (*The Message*). Thus St. Paul exhorted the earliest Christian community in his writing to the Romans two millennia ago. This exhortation was important for the early church and it is urgent for the Episcopal Church to heed as it enters the twenty-first century. Be transformed. Be changed from the inside out.

Perhaps no term fits the work and circumstances of the church in the twenty-first century better than "transformation." We are increasingly aware of the need for change as we become ever more mission-focused in the life of the church, both internationally and domestically. But society as a whole is rapidly moving in new directions, and mission cannot be embraced in an unexamined way, relying on old cultural and ecclesiastical stereotypes and assumptions.

This new series, *Transformations: The Episcopal Church in the 21st Century,* addresses these issues in realistic and hopeful ways. Each book focuses on one area within the Episcopal Church that is urgently in need of transformation in order for the church to be effective in the twenty-first century: vocation, evangelism, preaching, congregational life, getting to know the Bible, leadership, Christian formation, worship, and stewardship. Each volume explains why a changed vision is essential, gives robust theological and biblical foundations, offers guidelines to best practices and positive trends, describes the necessary tools for change, and imagines how transformation will look.

In this volume David Gortner, Assistant Professor of Pastoral Theology and Director of the Center for Anglican Learning and Leadership at the Church Divinity School of the Pacific, takes on the topic of evangelism in the Episcopal Church, asking: How can Episcopalians reclaim evangelism as an enriching spiritual practice? How soon will we recognize that our traditional hands-off approach has led to a crisis of faith with our own children? How will we learn to practice evangelism in a multicultural and multifaith society—and to what purpose? What styles and practices of spirituality enrich our sense of evangelical calling? This volume offers ways for every congregation to develop a climate and a plan for transformed evangelism. Like Christians in the early church, today we live in a secular culture that can be apathetic and even hostile to Christianity. Living in a setting where people are not familiar with the message or narrative of Christian believing requires new responses and new kinds of mission for the Body of Christ. We believe this is a hopeful time for spiritual seekers and inquirers in the church. The gospel itself is fresh for this century. God's love is vibrant and real; God's mission can transform people's hopes and lives. Will we participate in the transformation? Will we be bearers and agents of transformation for others? Will we ourselves be transformed? This is the call and these are the urgent questions for the Episcopal Church in the twenty-first century.

But first, seek to be transformed. Fix your attention on God. You'll be changed from the inside out.

JAMES B. LEMLER,
series editor

Acknowledgments

Writing this small volume on evangelism as a spiritual practice born of our immense gratitude has enriched my own Christian life and ministry. I am grateful for the persistence and encouragement of James Lemler and Cynthia Shattuck, who invited me to write this book, and for Cynthia's guidance as an editor.

For fourteen years I have been collecting stories and perspectives on evangelism, through pastoral experiences and the studies I have conducted or helped to conduct. My experiences in ministry have contributed immensely to my perspectives on evangelism. Many thanks to Tripp Hudgins, Larry Kamphausen, and Jane Schmoetzer for the work we shared in our ecumenical church-plant in Chicago with Church of Jesus Christ, Reconciler. The fifteen other congregations, campus ministries, and medical care facilities where I have served and learned have all been wonderful crucibles of formation, creativity, and passion—and the places where some of the stories in this book took shape.

Other stories came from prior research. My long-term study in twelve faith communities that have attracted people in their twenties and thirties laid the foundation for my development of processes for evangelistic listening. The stories of Theology on Tap from Chicago and the Episcopal campus ministry at SUNY-Buffalo come directly from this study. I am thankful to John Cusick, Kate DeVries, Kevin Sandburg, and Linda Wilson, and to the many young adults from these ministries (whose names have been changed). Stories and insights from a national study of Episcopal clergy leadership and congregational vitality, undertaken with John Dreibelbis, are woven into the fabric of this book, as are further insights on the personal theologies of young adults drawn from my dissertation.

In addition, for this book I interviewed clergy and lay leaders in other communities where I learned of strong evangelistic work. Their stories are the greatest strength of this book, and I am grateful to Bob Hernandez, Bishop Victor Scantlebury, Gary Cox, Hollis Wright, Bishop Bob Fitzpatrick, Susan Sherard, Kaze Gadaway, Mary Wilderman, Rich Melheim, Deb Streicher, Bonnie Perry, and Chuck Treadwell, as well as to others whose names have been changed.

I am grateful for the time, space, and support of my colleagues at Church Divinity School of the Pacific, especially John Kater and Linda Clader, who read draft chapters and offered their comments.

My father and step-mother, Robert and Jane, my in-laws, James, Joan, and Stewart, and my siblings have given constant encouragement and love. My mother, Aileen, before she died, placed in me the mark of her passion for God and for the Christian faith. And my beloved Heather has patiently and constantly supported my work on this book, reading drafts, discussing ideas, and giving me time and space. For all of those who continue to open the good news of Christ to me, and for the counsel, awakening, passion, teaching, and expansion of imagination I have received, I give thanks.

chapter one

"Go Therefore and Make Disciples"

Go therefore and make disciples of all nations, baptizing them in the name of the Father and of the Son and of the Holy Spirit, and teaching them to obey everything that I have commanded you. (Matthew 28:19–20a)

Evangelism is your natural expression of gratitude for God's goodness. Gratitude and wonder, born of grace, drive evangelism, propelling you outward beyond yourself to places you have not gone before. Your story compels you to give yourself to others, expressing in word and deed the wonder and delight of God's love for you and all humanity. In the process of offering your stories and hearing the stories of other, you help create new community. After hearing Jesus name her honestly and without reproach, the Samaritan woman is so amazed that she runs to tell others about her encounter. She doesn't have eloquent words—she is simply straightforward about her experience, and asks a question of the heart: "Come and see a man who told me everything I have ever done. He cannot be the Messiah, can he?" (John 4:29).

Go. Make disciples. Baptize. Teach. These are highly active words. Jesus invites his disciples, stunned and giddy with wonder and joy, up onto a mountain at the boundaries of their known world to witness his departure and to look beyond their own horizons. There, he invites them further into the pilgrimage of evangelistic life: to spread good news, to find kindred souls and searchers for God wherever they go, to share their stories of encounter with Jesus, and to bring people the promise of new life and enduring love in God.

Evangelism is a spiritual practice: active—and receptive. Just as in prayer, study, and acts of compassion, in evangelism you experience a sense of your movement not being entirely your own. Receptive to the Holy Spirit's activity within you—and trusting that the Spirit is active in others all around you—you move into action as the Spirit's partner. You become actively attuned to seeing and celebrating the presence of Christ already at work in the lives of others before you arrived on the scene. Energized by your active and practiced gratitude for all that you have received as gift from God, you enter your public life daily with a readiness to share your gratitude and wonder with others—and to hear their own experiences of God's abundant goodness. This kind of evangelism, the giving of your delight, returns to you abundantly as you are nurtured and strengthened by listening for and sharing good news.

True evangelism emerges only out of your own transformation. Your message of hope, of abiding faith, of joy—your "song of love unknown"—can only become natural, free, and open when you recall for yourself those moments of rescue, reorienting, awakening, and invigoration that are the result of God's work within and around you.

It is your stories of personal transformation that make evangelism possible. They are the source of energy propelling you toward others with the urgency of gratitude and wonder. Fear slips away as you trust, and then learn, that God is working in others like God has worked in you—that transformation is happening or ready to happen all around you. The practice of evangelism grows stronger as you allow the Spirit to awaken in you the love of others that God already has for them. It continues to transform you and your perceptions of the world as you willingly embrace a discipline of listening in a new way to people in your everyday encounters.

This book attempts to offer a new understanding of evangelism—not as a duty to be performed but as the practice of expressing our delight and wonder at the work of God. Evangelism is not something to be institutionalized or programmed, but is the work of individuals and communities bearing witness to Christ in their own unique ways. Evangelism is not something one simply does *to* another for another's sake, but is a spiritual discipline that nurtures and transforms the one who bears good news and recognizes God at work in others.

Unfortunately, since rejecting the religious passion roused by George Whitefield, John Wesley, Devereux Jarratt, and other leaders of the First Great Awakening in the eighteenth century, the Episcopal Church has never been comfortable with evangelism outside of foreign mission. We inherited some of our reticence from the Church of England, which, although supportive of foreign mission at different points in its history, has its own history of resistance—until recently—to the ideas and practices of evangelism. And in the religious culture surrounding us, we sometimes see and hear examples of ugly and unhappy evangelism, motivated by guilt rather than gratitude, delivered with arrogance rather than humble mutuality, and offered through canned rhetoric and emotional manipulation rather than genuine, heartfelt human story. But evangelism doesn't have to be this way. For a change of mind and habit to take place, we must first understand the assumptions that have both directly and indirectly undermined evangelism, and begin to identify those practices that have engaged evangelism effectively in the Episcopal Church. This will take self-recognition on our part. It will also require a scriptural and theological reimagining of evangelism—a new vision of what evangelism might be—with the assurance that others are already practicing this kind of evangelism and that we can indeed learn something new.

I hope that this book can in some small way help to transform our habits of evangelism. In this chapter, we will examine the Episcopal Church's attitudes to evangelism and its implicit and unquestioned barriers to personal evangelistic work. In chapter two, we will seek a new theological vision for evangelism that follows the leading of the Holy Spirit in a holy pilgrimage that recognizes the Spirit's work in our own lives and in the lives of those we meet. We will then hear in chapter three the stories of real people and real faith communities that have actually embraced evangelism as a spiritual practice. An array of exercises follows in chapter four that will encourage the development of spiritually grounded evangelistic habits. And in the final pages we will consider several ideas and images for our future as fellow pilgrims together, embracing the practices of individual and interpersonal evangelism rooted in the hearing and sharing of stories as part of the great and continuously unfolding story of God's redemptive work.

---

two stories

I grew up a "mongrel Christian"—the child of Lutheran parents, one American Lutheran (which later became part of the ELCA), the other Missouri Synod. A few years after my baptism as an infant, my parents left their Lutheran heritage behind, and we embarked as a family on a spiritual pilgrimage through multiple denominations—Methodist, Presbyterian, Christian and Missionary Alliance, Presbyterian (again), and Evangelical Mennonite. Our spiritual sojourn at times coincided with geographic relocation, as we left our Pennsylvania origins and followed my parents' unfolding careers and callings to New Jersey and then Indiana. There, during high school, and a few years later in college in Illinois, I began playing piano and organ in various churches—United Brethren, Roman Catholic, and, finally, Episcopal.

The small Episcopal mission church where I played was a bit "lackluster" in appeal when I started there. But over a period of four short years, I saw tremendous, steady transformation of spirit from a weary and somewhat embittered community to a fellowship of energy, exuberance, and deep and joyful celebration of faith. The change of heart I saw in people struck me deeply, and I found people who were profoundly genuine about their faith in God and who celebrated the love of Christ, while still being very real and honest about who they were as human beings.

Nonetheless, despite such a positive experience of congregational renewal, this Episcopal mission community expressed an unwavering aversion to the word "evangelism." Members were happy to reach out to people who entered the doors of the church—but they did not warm up to the idea of bearing their life of faith out into public places and speaking to people in the surrounding community. Across the slow-moving muddy river behind the church sat a large apartment complex. Our new vicar, along with several of us, suggested to church leaders and choir members that we set aside time to go meet people in the apartment complex, talk to them about our growing joy in the Christian life, and invite them to our church. The responses ranged from quizzical silence to a noncommittal

"Oh, that's interesting" to outright resistance. I will never forget one choir member's words: "Why do we need to talk to people in the neighboring apartment complex? They can see the church plainly—if they are interested or curious, they will come."

Another story. A few years ago, when I was leading a workshop on young adult ministry in an eastern diocese, Sarah, a high school senior, spoke up and told us how her church had dismissed her interest in forming a congregation-based young adult ministry. Sarah was clearly dedicated to her church and devoted to her faith; she was delighting in a vibrant high school youth ministry. She and her friends had participated regularly not only in her local youth group, but in diocesan events, camps, and the national Episcopal Youth Event. Her church also had a definite commitment to ministry with and by its youth, and to the raising up of young leaders in the church: Sarah was a full voting member of the parish vestry and worked alongside other lay people in supporting and strengthening the ministries of the congregation.

Sarah wanted the dynamic fellowship of her peers to continue beyond high school. She came to the vestry with a proposal: to create a post-high school, young adult ministry group that would allow young people to continue their journeys together and to support one another in the faith. "I had had this great experience, and I looked down the road and saw that there was nothing for us as young adults after high school. I wanted the church to help us create something." Sarah was surprised by the vestry's lack of enthusiasm. But she was even more surprised when a late middle-aged woman on the vestry responded, "Oh, honey, this is the time when you will go away for a time, and have adventures, and do some things you might regret. And then you'll come back, and we'll forgive you, and we will all be together again."

These two stories exemplify some common assumptions and habits that undermine our efforts in evangelism in the Episcopal Church. In the first story, good Episcopalians limited themselves to the common assumption of "red door evangelism": "If we paint the door red, then people will notice what a beautiful red door we have, and they will be curious and come inside to find out what it is all about." This passive means of engaging in evangelism ignores the active response Jesus asked of us in the first clause of the Great Commission: "*Go* and *make* disciples." The second story makes explicit a common assumption of older church members regarding upcoming generations: "Sure, young people will leave for a time and rebel against church, but they will come back when they are more settled—perhaps when they are married, but surely when they have children, a mortgage, and pledge-able income." More pointedly, this story betrays an underlying *laissez-faire* tradition of evangelism with upcoming generations that dismisses the last clause of the Great Commission: "*Teach* them."

---

the mis-practice and non-practice of evangelism

During the heyday of mainline Protestantism in the mid-twentieth century, churches grew quickly—more people came to church, more people joined, more programs were developed, and membership and involvement in a religious community was not only widely accepted but expected in American society. The growth curve reached its peak during the decade following World War II, when many denominations engaged in programs of rapid expansion and vigorous new member recruitment. And at first, people responded. They came, joined, and participated in religious communities—with widely varying degrees of interest, understanding, or investment in Christian life and faith. And mainline denominations enjoyed a sense of social prominence, respect, and public influence.

Episcopal churches participated in this general campaign of growth while continuing a long-standing pattern of "habitualized institutional Christianity"—concluding that people would perpetually sustain their denominational allegiance, and that denominational membership was essentially the same as Christian commitment. Two assumptions prevailed: 1) We are an American religious institution and part of the identity of what it means to be American; 2) Our unique culture of habitual expressions of religious life will continue from generation to generation, as our children carry on the traditions we ourselves inherited or created.

When church people start talking about putting people in the pews, they're already speaking the language of decline. If our focus is to receive the life God is to give us, and live that transformed life, the question of evangelism takes care of itself. — *Bishop Marc Andrus*

Bishop Claude Payne and Hamilton Beazley discussed the "maintenance model" of Christian community in their book *Reclaiming the Great Commission,* pointing out how the union of church and empire locked the church into a maintenance model that has continued since the time of Constantine. This "maintenance" approach to congregational ministry in the preindustrial and early industrial periods was perhaps legitimate. For centuries church membership had been geographically defined by residence in nearby neighborhoods and communities (what Anglicans and Roman Catholics called "the parish"). Religious identity was closely tied to cultural or ethnic identity, and adult children were more likely to settle in homes near their parents and thus more likely to continue attending the church of their birth.

But in the face of ever-increasing social mobility, steadily declining membership, and decreasing denominational loyalty, the "maintenance" approach is no longer tenable, and the church is slowly but steadily moving to adopt a "mission" approach to ministry. As we move into the twenty-first century, a number of dioceses, congregations, and ministries in the Episcopal Church are working to adopt a more mission-oriented approach to our religious life.

However, the institutional habits of generations continue to perpetuate a low regard for evangelism. Many of my lay and ordained colleagues in the Episcopal Church still wince at the word "evangelism," as it conjures up images of televangelists, mean-spirited street preachers, incendiary Jack Chick tracts, and Jehovah's Witness missionaries knocking at one's door. The maintenance approach over generations and centuries has produced a "why bother?" mentality, and the habitualized church has left the institutionalized faithful with little language or practice for articulating their faith and relationship with God to other human beings outside—and sometimes even inside—the walls of the church.

Mainline churches have not always helped parents learn how to transmit Christian faith to their children, and have often taken a *laissez-faire* approach to both adolescent and adult Christian formation. As a result, many have left the Christian traditions of their youth, including the Episcopal Church; lacking friendly help, comparably fewer have found a different Christian tradition. Moreover, such churches maintain these mis-practices and non-practices of evangelism through the help of some supporting myths:

+ People will come if they are interested—after all, we are a destination church.

* Children will be formed as Christians simply through participation in the weekly rituals and teachings of the church.

* Young people are *supposed to* leave, to sow their wild oats; they will return when they are ready to settle down.

These myths are not true, and they are a touch arrogant. People will not show up to a hidden community. Even though children are certainly prepared to ask big questions, tell and hear stories, learn how to pray, and think about God and life and good and evil, too often their parents do not know how to nurture their child's developing spirituality at home. As for youth and young adults, across generations there has indeed been a strong tendency to disengage and even to leave the faith traditions of childhood, with the greatest exodus immediately after high school. This exodus and disengagement was noted as early as the 1920s, and has been clearly documented in Wade Clark Roof's research on the baby boomer generation. It occurs across denominations, but is highest among the mainline traditions. Roof found that about 60 percent of boomers raised in a faith tradition left, and less than half of those returned to their own denomination (or to another denomination)—a trend that has continued with subsequent generations.[1] Now, after several generations of progressive attrition, more and more people have grown up with no religious affiliation and no connection with the central sacred stories and ideas that form Christian religious consciousness.

Evangelism in the twenty-first century will require both primary evangelism and continuing evangelism. *Primary evangelism* involves bringing the good news of God's love to people who have never heard the stories—and, as cultural familiarity with the core Christian stories diminishes with each new generation, this challenge

Evangelism is a Spiritual pratic

increases. *Continuing evangelism* involves direct and regular engagement on matters of Christian faith with our children and youth in our own and one another's households, even more importantly than in our church buildings. This dual focus may or may not help us save ourselves as a denomination—a misplaced motivation in itself—but it will help us embrace evangelism as a deeply invigorating spiritual practice that touches our waiting world—and our waiting children.

Evangelism in the twenty-first century will require us to become more comfortable naming the One who is the Source of Life within and among us. This means becoming adept at telling our own stories of transformation and at hearing others' moments of encounter with God that they may not even recognize as holy moments. It will involve us in discovering new languages, expressions, and ways of engaging with others who are not like us. It will involve us in learning—or re-learning—how to express more freely our passion for and gratitude to God as individuals. Most fundamentally, it will draw us away from over-reliance on the institutional church to do the work of evangelism for us, and invite us to lay claim to our Christ-given right to proclaim God's goodness in speech and action, as our spiritual discipline of expressing gratitude for Love's redeeming work in our own lives.

This will be quite a stretch for Episcopalians!

what episcopalians have thought . . . really

"Evangelism": it is a strangely uncomfortable word for mainline Christians, and especially for Episcopalians. Some refer jokingly to the "E-word," laughingly acknowledging a feeling that "evangelism" is a dirty word. Consistently, when I ask people at churches and diocesan events what images come to mind with the word "evangelism," I hear negative ideas such as "someone telling me what to believe," "slick hairdo's," "Bible thumpers," "pushy, in-your-face tactics," or "it's all about how guilty you are or how we are in and you are out." Such negative images repel many Episcopalians, providing an easy escape from really engaging Jesus' challenge to proclaim good news.

During the past fifty years there have been three general stances toward evangelism among members and leaders of the Episcopal Church:

1) Please don't mention the word again.

2) We prefer to engage in "silent witness."

3) We need only bring people into contact with our institutions of worship and ministry programs—the magic will then happen naturally.

A kind of "allergy" to the concept of evangelism has infused the Episcopal Church with habitual avoidance of and discomfort with the word itself at all levels of church functioning. The word "evangelism" is absent from both the Outline of Faith and the ordination services in the Book of Common Prayer. Episcopal seminaries have rarely, if ever, offered courses in evangelism. There are no entries for "evangelism" in core reference books for church leaders such as the *Westminster Oxford Dictionary of Ethics* and the *Oxford Dictionary of the Christian Church*, and the word appears only rarely in books written by leading Episcopal and Anglican theologians.

Another symptom of allergy is the apologetic tone we hear in those few sermons, conferences, and workshops in which evangelism is the focus. In 1999, for example, I helped coordinate and lead a lay training conference on evangelism in a midwestern diocese. We spent close to an hour discussing people's sensitivities to the word and how we should title the conference; the planning team finally settled on "The In's and Out's of the 'E-word.'" In 2004, a bishop in a western diocese preached at a convocation on evangelism, reassuring people that they didn't actually have to *tell* anyone about their personal faith, but simply invite them to church. Other bishops have adopted a focus on "deeds-based evangelism," validly emphasizing the proclamation of God's redeeming love through our actions as Christians, but also permitting acts of charity and social advocacy to substitute for the equally necessary evangelistic work of hearing and speaking.

> Changing to a new religious orientation takes place through what sociologists call kinship and friendship networks of one sort or another.... People who convert or change religions usually do so through personal contact, and not through impersonal methods.
> — *Lewis Rambo*

To be fair, many Episcopalians have developed tremendous practices of relational evangelism and evangelism by example. Warm and generous acts of hospitality and new member incorporation introduce parish newcomers to the experience of grace expressed in community. Individuals and churches deeply committed to living the Baptismal Covenant in lives of devotion to the apostles' teaching and service to neighbors and society indeed bear witness in their actions to God's work in their lives. Newcomers to those vibrant communities experience the best kind of "evangelism by osmosis," as these congregations naturally live out their new habits and communicate their deep life of faith without anxiety or apology. For people whose life journeys have been marked by abuse, hostility, neglect, or deception, such experience of a different kind of human community is indeed good news.

But there are shortcomings to relational evangelism and evangelism by example. In isolation, these strategies can allow individuals and congregations to drift too easily into habits of insularity and inarticulateness, as people engage and form relationships only with others "like us" and, because of a false division of word from deed, develop an aversion to naming for others the Source of the hope within them. Furthermore, evangelism by example presumes that Christians will be noticed as somehow different (in other words, "spiritually superior") from other kind, loving, and grace-gifted human beings, sparking people's curiosity so that they will ask us why we behave as we do. This *may* happen; but to count on such a response presumes that Christian acts of kindness and patterns of life are somehow more virtuous or noticeable than those of others—a presumption others are not likely to share. Moreover, we do ourselves, others, and the gospel a disservice when we presume that such observation and curiosity will simply happen as a matter of course and thus resort to verbal passivity.

An over-reliance on evangelism by example and relational evangelism also places the primary responsibility for evangelism on the institutional church, assuming that its manifold programs will do the heavy lifting of direct proclamation. But direct proclamation falters at the level of the local parish when programs substitute a kind of passive "evangelism by osmosis"—fostering a parishwide reliance on "worship as evangelism," "social ministry as evangelism," "inclusivity as evangelism," and "orthodoxy as evangelism." Yes, each of these approaches offers real strengths of the Episcopal Church, and bears witness to our love of Christ and our life in the Spirit. People have indeed found or rediscovered their faith in God by absorbing experiences in our worship, our social outreach, our welcome of all people, and our commitment to Christian teaching in its many variations. But reliance on these different forms of "evangelism by osmosis" allows us as individuals and communities to escape responsibility for direct evangelism—and so we fail to fulfill our complete baptismal vow to "proclaim by *word and example* the Good News of God in Christ."

a g l a n c e a t o u r s e l v e s n o w

For over thirty years now, mainline denominations have been noting, lamenting, and mulling over their numeric decline. While I do not wish the topic of evangelism as a joyful spiritual practice to be hijacked by concerns for reversing institutional decline, it may be valuable for us to have an accurate picture of our past and current place in the American religious landscape.

> Why is the Episcopal Church declining in numbers, and why are our serious efforts at evangelism so few and far between? — *W. Taylor Stevenson*

According to Kirk Hadaway's review of church data, in 1930 the number of baptized members in the Episcopal Church was just under 2 million. By 1966, this number was over 3.6 million. By 2005, membership was again below 2 million. The most precipitous decline occurred between the mid-1960s and the early 1980s, when youth and young adults of the Baby Boomer and early Generation X cohorts made their exit, never to return. While some scholars have come to view the 1950s and early 1960s as a "blip" in our cultural history, a time of heightened need for and interest in institutional affiliations, it is also clear that until around 1966, the Episcopal Church was keeping apace with general population increases, still holding roughly 2 percent of the American population as members. Now, our membership accounts for less than 1 percent of the population nationally, with higher representation in only a few places in the country (including concentrations in the northeast and mid-Atlantic regions, and scattered in the inner-mountain west). In fact, the only places in the country where Episcopal Church membership exceeds 8 percent of the population are in the Native American and Inuit nations—reflecting the heritage of some strong mission efforts in the 1800s and early 1900s. These are also sparsely populated areas, and the local churches continue to struggle to raise up new leaders and sustain new generations in the faith.[2]

We can forecast further decline by looking at the current distribution of age in our congregations. Drawing on data from the Faith Communities Today study, James Lemler reports that age distribution in the Episcopal Church skews significantly older than the general population—and very few congregations reflect the age demographics of their surrounding communities. My colleague John Dreibelbis and I found an even starker pattern in our national study of congregational vitality and clergy leadership. When we matched each congregation's report to the census data of its surrounding community, we found significant age disparities, with young adults accounting for less than 7 percent of church attenders, and youth accounting for less than 8 percent.

We found even more significant racial and socioeconomic skewing. In general, the Episcopal Church still gravitates toward financial and social capital. Episcopal congregations that are thriving and growing are much more frequently in upper-middle and upper class suburbs, and to a lesser degree in urban areas situated in neighborhoods where wealth was at least a prior, if not current, contributor to the church's security. Episcopal congregations with the highest attendance and most financial resources—and thus, most often the best resources for children—are typically in communities with fewer children and smaller families. True, there are many growing congregations across the country, and some in surprising contexts, but they are unfortunately outpaced by membership decline and stagnation in many more congregations. As a denomination we look less and less like the population surrounding us, with over 60 percent of our congregations in communities where the general population has remained 75 percent or more Caucasian. This reality simply reflects our institutional heritage: we built churches to minister to English-Americans; we served landowners, government leaders, and industry giants, and became a destination church for upwardly mobile Protestants; we built schools that became elite institutions; and in worship and manner of fellowship we became what sociologist Emile Durkheim described as a society celebrating an idealized image of itself.[3]

> It has been very hard for liberal Protestants to get over the fact that we don't run things anymore.
> — *William McKinney*

It is also no accident that most of our clergy do not have skills in evangelism and decisive leadership, charisma, or abilities to act as catalytic agents in their congregations—they were neither selected nor trained for those purposes. When asked what they felt most confident doing, rectors and vicars noted high confidence in being a role model, offering beautiful liturgies, and preaching well—but they were least confident in rebuilding congregations, developing relationships in the surrounding community, fostering strong lay leadership, and reaching out to lapsed members and unchurched people. They did not learn these skills in seminary, nor from their mentors or diocesan leaders.[4]

Habits run deep, and blame does not lie solely with any single group—laity, clergy, seminary professors, diocesan leaders, bishops, or the national church staff. In a number of congregations and dioceses, some groups are eager to see and do things differently but are not equipped with the right questions; other groups are so concerned with preservation of identity that they are unable to ask key questions of themselves. It has also been noted that members of Episcopal congregations more frequently mention concerns for membership growth than for helping people develop spiritually and find fuller life as Christians. We are a deeply institutionalized people—and our institutional habits and assumptions get in the way of more effective evangelism.

We should not underestimate the consequences of these unexamined institutional habits. Youth are particularly attuned to whether or not faith seems real to people. Christian Smith's national study of youth revealed that, compared to youth in other denominations, Episcopal youth hold less positive views of the church and consequently of their own faith. Our youth lead the mainline pack in uncertainty about God and infrequency of discussions of faith at home or in school, as well as in sensing that the church does not help them think about important things. Furthermore, they exceed all groups—even youth who are unaffiliated with any religion—in regarding adults in their church as hypocrites and as unapproachable.[5] Another study of incoming college students shows that Episcopal emerging adults exceed most other Protestant denominations in their religious disengagement.[6] Exodus from the church reaches its peak in the college and immediate post-college years, with few remaining and few returning. The pattern repeats and steadily increases with each generation. And the church diminishes.

Youth are quick to notice [passion's] absence in the church, quick to recognize the inwardness and awelessness of self-preservation. — *Kenda Creasy Dean*

What contributes to such attrition? We can get a good picture from looking at data on what contributes to strong retention and growth. Rodney Stark, in his book *The Rise of Christianity,* suggests that the church's rapid growth in the third and fourth centuries was not the result of a dramatic cultural shift, but rather followed the natural growth curve of a new religion that makes strong affirmations of what it stands for, commits its families and churches to fostering faith in upcoming generations, offers a breadth of appeal across social class, and shares leadership. Similar patterns can be seen in the Mormon faith and, interestingly enough, among the Amish. Attrition is more likely to occur when people don't know why they belong to a group or what it stands for, upcoming generations are not vigorously supported or encouraged in faith, membership and interest gravitate to particular subsets of society (by class, race, ethnicity, or age), and there are few places for people to offer their gifts and grow into leadership. In this kind of situation, rising generations leave altogether, find other faiths, or seek in a variety of ways to reclaim and rediscover their faith, often without adequate support or permission.

Class and race have been consistent barriers to widespread evangelism by the Episcopal Church. With the exception of a few missionary bishops, particularly among Native Americans, the Episcopal Church on the whole was late in westward movement, arriving once railroads had been built and town centers had been created. Support for evangelism and ministry development in working class communities has been sporadic, as it has been for our Asian, African-American, Latino, and Native American congregations. By the 1870s, the Episcopal Church had a little over fifty thousand black church members, while Methodist and AME churches had around half a million. The Episcopal Church was unable to rise to the cross-cultural challenge of ministry with Asian peoples from across the Pacific Rim, and our reach pales in comparison with Presbyterians, Methodists, and Baptists. Similarly, our ministry with Latino people continues in many places to falter and lag far behind other denominations, as we perpetuate a *noblesse oblige* mindset similar to that expressed in the 1800s in ministry among the lower classes and non-white communities: a superior attitude toward those we were "raising up" to respectable religion and societal responsibility.

True, there have been remarkable—if scattered— examples of primary and continuing evangelism in the Episcopal Church over the past two hundred fifty years. Individuals like Virginian priest Devereux Jarratt, New York bishop John Henry Hobart, Nevada Chinese layman Ah Foo, and Alaskan missionary Annie Farthing have taken evangelism as a primary part of their Christian life, promoting a vigorous faith, persistent in bringing the gospel to a hungry world. Groups like the Freedman's Council, the Brotherhood of St. Andrew, the Episcopal Church Women, and the Canterbury Clubs on college campuses emerged to bring the gospel in word and deed to communities otherwise neglected by the church. But overall, the evangelistic ministries represented by these people and programs depict the nature of Episcopal evangelism—scattered, secondary, and idiosyncratic to the trajectory of the institutional church. Many brilliant efforts by individuals and groups, for a variety of reasons, lost energy and support from the institutional church or themselves shifted focus to other projects and political interests. The strongest elements to retain from these efforts are their grassroots emergence and their reliance on laity as well as committed clergy for passion and clear evangelistic intentions.

Once again, this is not a problem of institutional motivation. There is plenty of positive motivation in diocesan and national resolutions, in bishops' teachings, and in the advocacy and occasional funding by various groups. But most of these efforts have come from the top, in moments of rising above the institutional patterns of clergy and laity who have taken on, unreflectively, the mindsets and habits found across our church culture. And these efforts did not address the challenge of helping individuals cross both implicit and explicit barriers to connect, human to human, with others not like themselves.

institutionalizing change?

At one level, the Episcopal Church has attempted to raise the acceptability of evangelism for decades. At different points during the last eighty years, the church has tried to focus itself on the work of evangelism—attempting to enact institutional change through institutional means. As early as 1925 the Commission on Evangelism appealed to the National Council of the Episcopal Church to make evangelism its central focus. The Bishops' Crusade of 1927 brought together clergy and lay people to refocus and enliven their Christian dedication. Some efforts were made at preaching missions—although one popular book of this movement urged a view that evangelism was best done by people participating in church programs.[7]

In 1948, the Lambeth Conference issued a set of resolutions and teachings. Among its many institutional focuses on responding to human rights, war, governments, political systems, and ecumenical relationships with other institutional church bodies, it also offered a set of resolutions on education, evangelism ("The Church Militant"), and discipleship ("The Christian Way of Life"). Resolutions on education focused on institutional solutions and challenges, but did not mention the work of parents with their children. Resolutions on evangelism urged lay members to rededicated service by strengthening "the corporate life and worship of their Church, and so to increase its influence upon the life of the community," and they placed the most central responsibility for evangelism with the clergy. The laity was asked to shoulder responsibility for corporate witness through regular attendance, financial support, and service to the church, and was charged with spiritual practices of private prayer and study, following Christ's teaching in daily life, and "boldness of their spoken witness to their faith in Christ."[8]

In 2006, the General Convention of the Episcopal Church also issued a set of resolutions on evangelism. The first called for a "national consultation on methods and strategies identifying best practices to reverse the decline in mainline denominations." Others stated support and greater institutional recognition of campus ministries, placed significant responsibility on bishops to "cast a vision" of evangelism for each diocese, and called for people in "all orders of ministry to speak about what God is doing in their lives; invite others to worship; and seek to identify and develop practical resources for personal and congregational evangelism through the Church Center staff." Room for significant financial contributions was made to support church planting.

Comparing the Lambeth Conference of 1948 with the Episcopal Church's General Convention of 2006 on matters of evangelism, it appears that we continue to operate with the same assumptions, addressing the challenge with top-down methods designed to reinforce Episcopal allegiance and charging people with evangelistic responsibilities for which we have provided no training. If nothing else, we are consistent... or is it persistent? Perhaps if we try again, and redouble our efforts, we will end up with different results?

Episcopalians' efforts to muster interest and effort for evangelism has been marked by two major national initiatives in the last two decades. In the 1990s, the Decade of Evangelism succeeded, if in nothing else, in at least reintroducing the word "evangelism" into the church's everyday vocabulary and raising consciousness of our need to practice it. Michael Green notes that "nearly all the major churches in the world determined to mark the decade A.D. 1990–2000 by intensive evangelization,"[9] against a backdrop of sweeping worldwide metacultural change. The effort, skeptically regarded by many and largely unknown by others, yielded little in increased church attendance, but at least raised the possibility of talking about evangelism among church members. Since the year 2000, the church has offered the 20/20 Initiative—a vision of doubling our church size nationally and our congregations locally by the year 2020 through efforts at congregational revitalization. Some dioceses have taken this invitation and begun work in a top-down manner on church growth and evangelism.

These efforts are no match for the passionate institutional commitment to mission that characterized the tone of the Episcopal Church—and many other denominations—over a century ago, when our church sent missionary bishops, priests, and lay people westward across the opening frontier and to other parts of the world. Today, the church experiences chronic difficulties in bringing these large-scale initiatives into the local parish. Moreover, such initiatives do not adequately assist individuals and communities of faith to overcome their aversions and anxieties regarding evangelism or to develop habit-forming skills for evangelism.

> It is the nature of systemic decline to deny the decline itself. . . . Blame is directed outward as long as possible, blaming the culture, the national church, and enemy group, etc. When the denial can no longer be focused outward, blame focuses within the denomination with internal conflicts. — *Charles Fulton and Jim Lemler*

The problem with these contemporary initiatives is neither the idea nor the motivation. The problem is in the grassroots application. Grand visions and lofty aims do not automatically yield results. The work of application is the "black hole" in such grand church proposals, leaving individuals and congregations frustrated with their own inability to meet the lofty goals placed before them—even with the plethora of printed and web-based materials available from the institutional church for them to digest. But there are deeper, more persistent problems that undermine the initiatives, such as the inadequate help offered by the institutional church to individuals and congregations for overcoming aversions and anxieties regarding evangelism and the lack of encouragement to embrace evangelism as a spiritual discipline. Still, tools are available. *Groundwork,* a resource designed to help congregations and dioceses more clearly identify opportunities for growth, outreach, and hospitality, begins to put some tools into the hands of clergy and laity at local levels as they attempt to work toward the goals of the 20/20 Initiative, though it doesn't deliver the hands-on training necessary for people to become effective evangelists.

We are meant to strive toward the theological ideal expressed by Archbishop William Temple when he called the church the only organization that exists solely for the benefit of those who are not its members. Without habits and tangible means for practicing this ideal, it remains just that—an ideal that feeds our guilt, defensiveness, and compulsive perfectionism but fails to connect with how we live our daily lives.

So, failure is not for a lack of will as much as for a lack of practice and practical guidance. We do not understand that evangelism is most fundamentally a spiritual practice of individuals connecting with their gratitude to God. Don't get me wrong: I am not trying to suggest that the institutional approach is somehow inherently sinful. I am simply saying that the institutional approach isn't working, and it is time to step back and try something else. Top-down evangelism is rooted in a medieval world-view, a world where the church was the mighty fortress, the city set on a hill beckoning all to itself from the outer darkness to what it alone could give light. In the continuing movement of our society and world toward a "flat earth" of "horizontal collaboration" and access to systems of influence, in the words of Thomas L. Friedman, this is not a sustainable *modus operandi*.

> I find even in small and very traditional churches a new hunger to reach out, matched by little understanding of how this might be attempted. — *Michael Green*

What is the approach that will work? Evangelism in the twenty-first century is:

+ Not a program, but a spiritual practice
+ Not institutional, but individual
+ Not for empire, but for public exchange
+ Not starting with telling, but starting with listening
+ Not "Come and See" without first "Show Me"
+ Not about citizenship, but about fellow pilgrimage
+ Not of or for the church, but of and for the Holy Spirit.

the church growth movement

For many evangelicals the birth of the Church Growth movement in 1955 with the publication of Donald A. McGavran's *The Bridges of God* was a watershed. The author, drawing on his missionary experience, developed and tested models for church growth and church planting while teaching at the Fuller School of World Mission in California. His work has been taken to heart by pastors like Bill Hybels at Willow Creek Community Church and Rick Warren at Saddleback Community Church, who are leading megachurches in different parts of the country. These churches have made unapologetic application of some of McGavran's core concepts: the pastor as central authority sets the vision and mission, and delegates concrete, contained leadership to assistant clergy and lay leaders; the leadership team targets specific constituencies of people and builds a vision and mission that speaks directly to the interests of those people, as much as possible in their own terms; the community is developed with intimate connection and discipleship in mind, using cell groups and covenant groups to build a faithful core community; and the church follows the benefits of reaching out almost solely to people who are like themselves. Interestingly, McGavran saw homogeneity as an evangelistic strength of a congregation, noting that "men [sic] like to become Christians without crossing racial, linguistic or class barriers."[10] Today's megachurches have become more ethnically diverse, as pastors have come to recognize the limitations of McGavran's ideas—but these churches tend to have multiple worship services that still target different groups.

The Episcopal Church (along with other mainline churches) has largely rejected this approach, ironically objecting to the hierarchical model of leadership and expressing a distaste for such an explicit push toward homogeneity. These may be sound theological objections, but our own institutional habits do not suggest that we are in a place to point the finger. On the other hand, the success of megachurches is directly related to social class— and the market approach to packaging the gospel in relevant terms can lead to an avoidance of issues that directly challenge people's deepest assumptions. Again, this is nothing new; it is the testament of institutional churches worldwide that they are, or were at one time, deeply responsive to their cultures, and that this responsiveness leads to some unfortunate accommodations.

Megachurch evangelism is still essentially institutional, relying on strategies handed down from the top, and depending on its Sunday morning proclamation in multimedia drama, song, and message to hook the seeker who dares to darken the door or who has responded to a friend's invitation. Lay leadership is developed, but with an eye toward helping to increase and build the institution—because building the institution is understood as building the kingdom of God, or vice versa. This institutional emphasis is the primary basis of criticism by the Emerging Church movement.

too true ↙

> Those churches that have been most creative and productive in their evangelistic efforts debate and write the least about it. They simply get on with the job. *—Cyril Okorocha*

Nonetheless, the dynamism and cultural responsiveness in the Church Growth movement can be instructive to the Episcopal Church. One finds the most positive applications of its insights among missionaries and evangelists working in more challenging settings. For example, Agnes Liu, a faculty member at Hong Kong's China Graduate School of Theology, worked in a clothes factory to learn first-hand about the culture of the working class, and then devoted sixteen years with her students to developing evangelistic ministries with workers. She learned that workers became open to Christianity when they got to know and like some Christians—after this, they became open to Christian worship and teaching. As a result of her work, hundreds of factory and service workers, as well as homeless and immigrants, have formed congregations that meet when people are most available, use symbols from their own lives, and rely heavily on peer-based evangelism.[11]

Primary and continuing evangelism require adjustment to a new world that has a wide range of audiences, including our own children and youth, lapsed or uncertain Christians, religious seekers, and those who are disconnected from religion. And so, effective evangelism begins with attention to a central question: *Who* needs to hear *what?*

In *Choosing Church* Carol Lytch outlines a continuum of religious identity for youth. Her categories can be helpful in thinking about the range of audiences for evangelism across all age-groups, including:

1) Those who have remained committed to the faith tradition in which they were raised (Conventionals, who never leave; Classics, who wrestle their way to commitment; and Reclaimers, who return after a time of absence);

2) Those who pick and choose parts of religious life and meaning for their own purposes (Marginalizers, who engage in the rituals but not the teachings; and Customizers, who pick and choose teachings they will embrace but reject the rest);

3) Those who have cast off the faith in which they were raised (Rejecters);

4) Those for whom all things religious are foreign and strange (The Lost).[12]

If we evaluate not only our congregations but our social communities and our overall American culture in light of these categories, we will likely be surprised at what a small segment of the population is represented by people with deep commitment to and conviction for their faith—and

— a spiritual practice
— radical listening
— individual
— transformational

at what a significant and growing proportion of the population is represented by those who have no knowledge of, negative reactions to, or little internalization of their faith. We will recognize that our renewed practices of hospitality and incorporation, while absolutely important, only touch a small fraction of the American public. The place of religion in the United States has changed—and continues to change.

Core Assertions for Evangelism in the Twenty-first Century

1) Evangelism is a spiritual practice of expressing gratitude for God's goodness and grace.

2) Both primary and continuing evangelism are the work of every generation with its surrounding culture and its own younger kindred and offspring.

3) Primary evangelism is the "new" challenge of twenty-first-century North America that calls for a deinstitutionalized approach.

4) Evangelism is and has always been first and foremost the work of individuals, not institutions or programs.

5) Evangelism begins with radical spiritual listening, proceeding from a respect of God's grace already present and active, rather than from a focus on God's absence and human deficit.

6) Evangelism necessarily involves both verbal exchange and action, has little place for privatism, and brings us into contact with people who aren't like us.

7) Evangelism is born of deep delight, often found in community, and feeding a community's vitality.

8) Evangelism transforms *us* in our communities and personal lives, as we recognize how wide and diverse are God's gifts and our understanding of those gifts.

This change in the American landscape is noteworthy—not just socially, but also religiously. Increasing ethnic diversity, along with diminishing interest in lifetime denominational loyalty, sets American citizens in an emerging context that favors multifaith experiences, a seeker orientation, and religious eclecticism. It is no surprise that the fastest growing category for religious affiliation selected on national surveys is "None."[13]

But there is more at stake than mere religious affiliation. These changes involve a reorienting of people's lives away from traditional religious concerns with the state of human souls and the strengthening of the common good. In a study undertaken for my dissertation at the University of Chicago, I discovered that over the past forty years, a dramatic change has taken place in the ultimate values young adults consider important. Young adults ages eighteen to twenty-five in this decade see happiness, family security, mature love, friendships, and self-respect as most important—and do not see salvation, social recognition, equality, and freedom as very important at all. They are not explicitly hedonistic (although they do value comfort, pleasure, and excitement more than the same age-group forty years ago). They are more concerned with personal development, most concerned with close and secure relationships—much more than young adults forty years ago—and, in relation to these other values, least concerned with broader spiritual and social concerns. It seems that more and more people today are becoming "marginalizers," if not "rejecters" of the traditional language of a Judeo-Christian society that was so strong not long ago.

This is not necessarily a change for the worse. It simply signals that we need to adjust our theological language—and we must do so by listening to where people's hearts are today. Shanille, one young adult in my study, told me, "My life in general needs to be a growth process. I try now to take every situation and learn something from it and grow from everything." When asked about people she admires, she said, "The people that are out there making a good world for themselves. And making a good world for everybody else. I admire the people the most who are doing everything in their power to make things better for them and everybody else." There are many possible connections between Shanille's values and a Christian understanding of life transformed by Christ—but the connections are not automatically through traditional church language or phrases like "the fear of the Lord."

To whom will we go? To whom will we speak? How shall we speak?

We are poised to make a significant change in our ways of doing evangelism in the Episcopal Church. The changes necessary will challenge and overturn some very deep habits and assumptions—including our impetus to look for top-down institutional solutions when the solution is within us as individuals and around us in our communities. The question is whether we will have the courage, humility, and enthusiasm to embrace such a change and make it part of our Christian identity.

evangelism: it's deeper than you think

Evangelism cannot be about church growth alone. If I locate the focus of my evangelism in a concern to increase the numbers of "butts in the pews," I have lost touch with gratitude and wonder as my motivations, and am now relying on collective anxiety.

*very
the*

Evangelism is, dare I say, remarkably unconcerned with the institution. It is concerned with human lives. Evangelism is not only being present in the community, living a wholesome public life, engaging in vigorous social ministry, advertising attractive church events, offering warm hospitality and welcome, or attempting to recruit new church members from the community. All these activities are secondary to something much more fundamental—the joyful spiritual practice of naming the Source of our gratitude and wonder.

Evangelism is fundamentally a spiritual practice, as important to our spiritual health as prayer, worship, fellowship, and study. As such, evangelism is not simply an act or a set of Christian techniques. It is not a programmatic effort or a formulaic recitation of a memorized speech. It is not a generation of false sentiments or a sale of artificial emotion. It is not wanton advertising of religious slogans. It need be neither demonstrative nor dogmatic. It is not recruitment. It is not judgment.

The belief that God wills the well-being of all calls forth the pivotal virtue of the moral life—gratitude.
— *Richard Gula*

True evangelism emerges from a practiced disposition of gratitude, a willfully embraced motivation arising from our experience of wonder, delight, and gratification in the Holy Spirit that propels us out to others to share our good news. And it is a new way of seeing and hearing others— as people who also have stories of delight and gratitude for God's movement in their lives. Evangelism is a willful, joyful spiritual discipline of seeing and naming the Holy Spirit at work in ourselves and those we encounter— giving voice to our own grace-filled experiences, and helping others find their voice. It is practicing what we read in the Psalms—no matter what our current state, we can recall for ourselves and others the great works of God in each others' lives.

Evangelism begins most fundamentally with you. On your holy pilgrimage you carry gifts for the world that are far deeper than you can even begin to recognize.

chapter two

"The Road to Jerusalem is in the Heart"

When I love you, my God, I want to embrace it all, for I love you with all my senses in the creations of your love. In all the things that encounter me, you are waiting for me.
— *Jürgen Moltmann*

To be genuinely Christian, any effort in evangelism must be grounded in a deep conviction of God's unbridled love for humanity and for all creation. An evangelism rooted in a theology of love, if really embraced, cannot help being evocative—and cannot help being expressed. The question is, whether or not we entrust ourselves to this Love.

> Something that creates a strong response or feeling

As sung in the Orthodox hymn, we know God as the Lover of humankind—by the very nature of our creation, by our day-to-day breath and existence, by our embrace in the forgiving and suffering arms of Christ. God loves what God has made—humanity in all its fractured, self-wounding, aggressive, creative, passionate, self-giving nature. God loves each person in the process of his own becoming, her own pilgrimage of life.

Evangelism is naming your own journey to love with the living God, wherever it takes you, and naming the presence of the Holy in the journeys of other people you encounter. From our first breath to our last, and beyond, God has set before each of us a pilgrimage. We each set out on a journey every day, stirred by a God-given restlessness and eagerness. The narratives of scripture, from the earliest Hebrew scriptures to the gospels, speak of many kinds of encounters with God. In the stories of Abram and Sarai, Ruth, Jonah, and most of all Jesus, we hear again and again how God's invitation stirs people out of passive corporate existence to live in new ways and new places.

I believe in kingdom come, when all the colors bleed into one.... But I still haven't found what I'm looking for. — *U2*, The Joshua Tree *album*

Unfortunately, when we—as laity or clergy—get fixated on or sucked into the work of preserving our parishes, expanding our sanctuaries, or making our programs run smoothly, we can begin to believe that this particular local church is our paradise, our final home. We forget our own pilgrimages and impose on the local church all our yearnings and expectations that it be the promised land we seek. We side-step the anxiety inherent in and the courage required for our own journeys by allowing ourselves to settle comfortably, forgetting that in joining Jesus, we too have become wayfarers.

Contemporary writers on evangelism and church life such as Robert Webber, Dorothy Bass, and Graham Tomlin have emphasized the need for an increased focus on personal discipleship—patterning one's life on following Jesus—rather than on corporate membership. Others, like Brian McClaren and Diana Butler Bass, talk about the need to leave behind "big" images of church and return to being companions to people on the road. Some of these writers recognize the deep inherent connection between mission

[Handwritten at top: Church should be not the end, but a step on the way, fellow travelers!]

and pilgrimage; they see that evangelism is not an invitation to "come home," but instead an invitation to "come on the Way with us." When we take this perspective, the corporate gathering or program no longer becomes the primary vehicle of evangelism or even the ultimate destination. Instead, the parish and its programs become places that support and strengthen committed pilgrims, or what Christian educator Parker Palmer in his book *Company of Strangers* has called "schools of the Spirit."

> Our word "parish" comes from the Greek *paraikos*,
> which means precisely "pilgrim, passing stranger."
> Is not every church, in fact, called to be the
> "pilgrim's house," centred on prayer and sharing?
> — Brother John of Taizé

The theme of pilgrimage lies deep within the biblical tradition. Abram and Sarai wandered for their entire lives as nomadic herders in the land of Canaan, following God's promise and pledging all they had to their relationship with God. Jacob and his son Joseph each met God in the midst of their desperate and untidy pilgrimages. Ruth left everything familiar to follow her mother-in-law into a foreign land. Jonah found himself on a journey he tried to avoid and encountered results that threatened to change him and his deepest assumptions. Jesus and his companions wandered the Judean and Canaanite countryside, faithfully attending the great pilgrim festivals in Jerusalem and meeting in synagogues, but constantly on the move. In Mark, one can imagine the disciples wanting to catch their breath as they tried to keep up with the fast-moving Jesus who had invited them to follow him on the Way. In John, Jesus the pilgrim Son of Man consistently pointed away from the fixed institutions of religion to a universe of truth and healing they had never yet encountered—in his own person.

[Handwritten in right margin: Wandering is a biblical theme]

Evangelism as journey and pilgrimage has also been a part of Christian thought and imagination, particularly *welcome to the pastures of today! ↓ !*

during times of cultural change, societal uncertainty, or religious upheaval. John Bunyan's *Pilgrim's Progress* remains a classic expression of the transformation of pilgrims who, in the company of wise guides, dare to follow a path to which the Holy Spirit compels them. *The Way of the Pilgrim* tells the story of a young Russian pilgrim in the nineteenth century who wandered from church to church looking for someone who could teach him to pray without ceasing. After frustrating encounters with any number of churches where he got no clear direction, he wandered until he found a hermit, who taught him how to pray.

C. S. Lewis likewise wrote in *The Pilgrim's Regress* about his own intellectual pilgrimage through the wastelands of the various philosophies of his day and his coming to baptism despite himself. Diana Eck's recent book *Encountering God* chronicles her own journey as a Christian, noting how encounters with faithful people from other religions transformed her relationship with God. In each of these books, the pilgrim continues to move, relentlessly—and in many cases, when the pilgrim rests too long in one place, trouble begins to stir. The pilgrim finds truth and discovers Love while on the road, in new places, and in conversation with people who dare to tell them their most sacred stories and to offer them what guidance they can.

Thus far did I come laden with my sin,
Nor could aught ease the grief that I was in,
Till I came hither: What a place is this!
Must here be the beginning of my bliss?
— *John Bunyan*, The Pilgrim's Progress

Each story of pilgrimage is unique. But we find in each story common themes of seeking and uncertainty, finding and being found, relief from burdens too heavy to bear, the gratification of discovering Love, and deep, transformative

- learning to trust God + Surrender to God in the midst of the insanity that constantly swirls around us is what will ultimately save us.

gratitude and wonder from that moment onward. And in each story we find that the moment (or moments) of transformation did not become the final resting place. Gratitude compelled the pilgrims to continue on their journeys, soon becoming guides for other pilgrims, and learning to trust the God who was their companion on the way, the ground of their pilgrimage, and the forerunner and lure of the race set before them.

> In this mortal life we can only travel by way of God's mercy and forgiveness, and they always lead us to his grace. — *Julian of Norwich,* Revelations of Divine Love

God is the One who meets us by our tents, who wrestles with us in the wilderness, who walks with us in the pledges of loyal friendship and in the discovery of love, who turns us around when we want to run. Most intimately in Jesus, God the creating Word joined us as a fellow pilgrim. Jesus' entire ministry was one of wandering and pilgrimage. His first act after baptism was not to settle into a congregation, but to wander and pray in the wilderness—driven there by the Spirit. When he returned from prayer and struggle, Jesus' next act was to seek out fellow travelers, inviting them to follow him without the promise of a clear destination. He himself was surprised along the journey, and found his own heart transformed by his encounters. When Jesus met the Syro-Phoenician woman, he was not immediately open to sharing his gifts of grace with her— but, in the midst of their conversation, Jesus found himself stunned by her faith, and changed his mind. When asked by a Roman military officer to heal his son, Jesus found himself in wonder and awe at the man's faith—"in no one in Israel have I found such faith" (Matthew 8:10). Jesus as a first-century Jew was not familiar with or interested in exploring the lives of foreigners, and so these encounters with eager, searching, and wise foreigners were for Jesus important moments of awakening, wonder, and transformation. This is one of the great mysteries of the God who gave up so much to become human and walk with us: in this great self-emptying, God yielded control and, in Jesus, was acted upon.

Pilgrims admit that they are wandering, not entirely clear about their next immediate destination but committed to following and finding the Love that like a star draws them on. Along the way they seek stories of sacred encounters from one another, to increase their travel-savvy, to expand and test and affirm one another's encounters, to learn better what to look for and what is possible. In the fourth century a nun named Egeria recorded in a journal her transformation in pilgrimage to Mount Sinai: "Though I had to go on foot I was not conscious of the effort—in fact I hardly noticed it because, by God's will, I was seeing my hopes coming true." Instead of returning to her convent, Egeria continued on her travels through Asia to Ephesus, sharing her wisdom and experience with her sisters back home. During Christianity's rise in Ireland following the missionary work of Patrick, Irish pilgrim missionaries embraced what came to be known as the "white martyrdom," leaving all things familiar in their lives and giving themselves over to "perpetual journeying for Christ."[14] The "martyrs" undertook their pilgrimages to create new faith communities, with a very deep conviction that Christ went behind, before, and beneath them, and that they would come to places where God intended them to be.

The element of uncertainty, which lies at the heart of both pilgrimage and mission, is nourished by the beckoning of God which calls us on. — Martin Robinson

From the twentieth century we have the examples of Jürgen Moltmann and Bishop K. H. Ting, theologians whose journeys led them on remarkable paths into places few of us will ever go. Moltmann walked with his German people through the dark shadows of horror, guilt, and shame after the atrocities of World War II. In a Scottish labor camp he discovered grace through the families who welcomed him and other prisoners into their homes, in the witness of Dutch students who spoke of Christ as the bridge that allowed them to cross over to their enemies, and in the Bible, where he found a Jesus who was his "divine brother in distress, who takes the prisoners with him on his way to resurrection."[15] Bishop Ting, the last remaining Anglican bishop in mainland China, walked with his people through the darkness of China's Cultural Revolution, maintaining a deep commitment to his belief in a humanity created in the image of God and the Holy Spirit's dwelling in all places and people in the world— including the people of his own nation's government whom most Christian communities around the world viewed with deep suspicion. These theologians have had remarkable impact on Christians across the globe.

> The way from alpha to omega is never a straight line, but love accompanies the pilgrims.
> — K. H. Ting, Love Never Ends

Pilgrims who trust God as the ground of all pilgrimage find that they become more highly attuned, more acutely aware of indicators of God's presence and activity. At the same time, there is an adventurous, slightly unnerving edge to this sense of pilgrimage; we cannot domesticate the untamed Christ who surprises us on the road. As C. S. Lewis's characters constantly reminded each other about the Christ-figure, Aslan, in the Narnia Chronicles, "He is not a tame lion." The certainty of God's presence and of encountering holy ground is paired in our pilgrim journeys with the riveting uncertainty of just how we will encounter Christ anew.

All mission—and, as a consequence, all evangelism— begins, proceeds, and ends with the Holy Spirit. So often we get it backward and assume that the church creates mission. We couldn't be more wrong, for it is the Holy Spirit's mission in the world that creates—and constantly re-creates—the church. And it is the Holy Spirit whose life-giving and awakening lure is present in all human lives long before we ever arrive as evangelists. This has been difficult for us as control-oriented humans to acknowl-edge, from the very beginnings of Christian history.

> John said to him, "Teacher, we saw someone casting out demons in your name, and we tried to stop him, because he was not following us." But Jesus said, "Do not stop him; for no one who does a deed of power in my name will be able soon after-ward to speak evil of me. Whoever is not against us is for us." (Mark 9:38–40)

Here we see Jesus' disciple John taking the first steps toward institutional religion. *If only we impose rules of membership on the exercise of ministry, then things will proceed in their just and proper course.* Jesus dismisses this misplaced allegiance, offering instead a far more expansive understanding of God's mission: *Whoever is not against us is for us. Their fruits will tell you something about the source of their power and ministry.* In this and other passages in the gospels, Jesus shatters the disciples' attempts to contain God's mission within specified limits.

The biblical narrative continues to unfold as a witness to the work of the Holy Spirit, in spite of early Christians' gravitation toward an institutionalization of the Way. Philip was practically dragged by the Holy Spirit to meet the Ethiopian on the road; then it was the Ethiopian who led Philip by showing him the scripture he was reading and asking to be baptized. Ananias, urged by the Holy Spirit to find Saul and pray with him, at first resisted because of Saul's persecution of Christians. But God said, "Go, for he is an instrument whom I have chosen to bring my name before Gentiles" (Acts 9:15). As for Peter, he needed even more blatant persuasion, not only through three dreams of unclean animals and God's invitation to eat them, but by the faith of those Gentiles gathered at the house of Cornelius, before he finally could say, "I truly understand that God shows no partiality, but in every nation anyone who fears him and does what is right is acceptable to him" (Acts 10:34–35). The apostles and believers back in Jerusalem were only hesitantly convinced by Peter, whose explanation for baptizing Cornelius and other Gentiles was rather apologetic: "'If then God gave them the same gift that he gave us when we believed in the Lord Jesus Christ, who was I that I could hinder God?' When they heard this, they were silenced. And they praised God, saying, 'Then God has given even to the Gentiles the repentance that leads to life'" (Acts 11:17–18). Only at this point did the church begin to welcome Gentiles. It is interesting to note that from this point onward in the Acts of the Apostles the church in Jerusalem recedes into the background as the centerpoint of the rapidly growing Christianity. By the end of the book, it becomes difficult to identify any real "center" of a Christianity that is seemingly forever on the move, riding on the tide of the Holy Spirit's movement.

Evangelism ≠ Conversion

At our best, we permit the Holy Spirit to take the lead, trusting that God is already at work in all people, allowing ourselves the possibility of being transformed by new encounters with God's grace among people who do not yet know the name of Jesus. An important but simple truth emerges from this trust in the Holy Spirit: *evangelism is not the same as conversion.*

Evangelism is allowing ourselves to come into contact with others and creating space in which God's good news can be told, shared, and revealed—the spiritual work of every Christian in cooperation with the Holy Spirit. Conversion is what happens inside as a person or group hears and digests stories of God's good news. Conversion is transformation, turning, the shift of will and motivation that happens in a person, family, or community—the work of deep, mutual, internal conversation between the Holy Spirit and the one coming to recognize Love's story. We simply serve as one possible catalyst among many catalysts.

There is an essential point to this little formula. Evangelism *is* about listening for and proclaiming stories of God's transforming message of love and delight—it is *not* about what happens as a result of our sharing these stories. We do not measure evangelism by outcomes or results. We cannot define our participation in the Holy Spirit's work of evangelism by counting the number of converts or the intensity of transformations in people's lives. In the words of missiologist David Bosch, "Evangelism is not the same as church extension."[16]

An uncomfortable corollary follows: we cannot say we are truly embracing evangelism as a spiritual practice just because our local church grows in attendance. Church growth or solid church programs may or may not be the result of our evangelism; people join churches and support programs for a host of reasons, going where they find joy and health—but moderate church growth is often simply due to population increases and socioeconomic changes in the surrounding community. This is good news because the fact that "it's not about the outcome" can free us from one of the crippling anxieties that prevents us from embracing evangelism as a joyful spiritual practice. When we withdraw from sharing good news because we are anxious about people's responses, we are staking too much on the outcome and we have lost focus on the heartfelt gratitude to God that motivates our sharing in the first place. It does not matter how people respond! It matters more that we are true to who we are, who we have been made to be, and who we are becoming in Christ—and that we live that truth openly, in words and deeds, in our sharing with others. The more we try to create what we want as the "right" response in another person or group, the more we risk drifting toward sales and manipulation. True evangelism involves living fully as a Christian in this present moment, speaking openly from one true self to another.

not about outcome

---

signs of the Spirit's presence

So how can we know that the Holy Spirit has been present and working with people before we arrive? After all, we can be remarkably oblivious to the signs of God's presence and movement in ourselves, in others around us, and in the communities in which we live and work. But we can learn to recognize signs in people's emotions, motivations, thoughts, and actions—the "fruits" of their lives. The more familiar we become with these signs in our own lives—the rich and varied moments of vibrancy, insight, joy, and wonder (and yes, also confusion and pain) that we encounter in everyday moments of our lives—the more attuned we will become to such moments in others' lives.

Some of the most central signs for us are Paul's "fruits of the Spirit": love, joy, peace, patience, kindness, generosity, faithfulness, gentleness, and self-control (Galatians 5:22). These fruits grow naturally from the life surging within. We notice the Holy Spirit moving in the *love* of family members and friends—even when it is distorted or one-

When experience forever changed HSP you are forever changed I cry tears of joy ☺

sided. We see the Holy Spirit's presence in the *joy* of smiles, laughter, and humor. We sense the Spirit's comfort in *peace* that finds us in the midst of deadlines, drudgery, and disease. God's Spirit is participating with us—and leading us—in our smallest and greatest moments of *kindness* and *generosity,* to ourselves as well as friends and strangers. In the teacher or coach waiting eagerly but patiently for a student to "get it," in the student's steady efforts in the face of frustration, in the young child learning that there are other ways besides tantrums to resolve conflict, the Holy Spirit is inviting and celebrating fruits of *patience, faithfulness,* and *self-control.* Paul's list is by no means exhaustive—one may find evidence of wisdom, courage, and just judgment in people's lives, and these "cardinal virtues" likewise came to be recognized by medieval theologians as God's mark.

Some Responses to Experiences of the Holy Spirit
+ Wonder, awe;
+ Rest, calm;
+ Turning, change, transformation;
+ Devotion, commitment;
+ Joy, gratitude;
+ Vigor;
+ New purpose.

This approach of finding, naming, interpreting, and celebrating the vibrant life of the Holy Spirit already present in people has become a central practice in evangelism and mission—with particular attention to unique expressions of the Holy in each culture. For instance, Bishop Ting invited the Protestant Church in China to embark with him on the adventure of what he called "reconstructing theology"—finding ways to help Christianity become truly indigenous by looking for the gospel's connections with Chinese culture and society. He saw signs of God's presence in the strong Chinese value of *harmonious living-with-others,* which included the integration of opposing ideas and forces—a pattern that was different from the heritage of Western philosophy, which emphasized categories and distinctions. In Nigeria today, Archbishop Akinola and other church leaders give voice to the deep cultural expressions of God they find in their people's commitments to honor and fidelity—even in the face of open hostility from Muslim communities from the north. Missionary accounts are full of rich examples of how missionaries succeeded in bringing the gospel to people when they entered deeply into their cultures and found signs of the Holy Spirit already at work. These accounts serve as correctives to the other unfortunate accounts of missionaries who failed to connect with people when they used the gospel as a bludgeon and viewed people's cultures with condemnation.

In our own society we may find signs of the Spirit in qualities such as *resilience* in the face of trauma, *determination* to live and thrive despite one's wounds and brokenness, and *self-honesty* that leads one beyond simplistic categories of victim and villain. In human qualities that pull us toward life, God's grace is active in the midst of our experiences of fracture and hurt. Even in people and circumstances in which we can find no such fruit, where all appears barren, the Holy Spirit is active—suffering and mourning the barrenness, groaning with all creation for a day of new birth and fresh rain, seeking to arouse life through the *sorrow, anger, fear,* or *disgust* that, paradoxically, signal to us that life might be better.

The fruits of the Spirit are born from energies deep within us (some call this source the "image of God"), are sparked by interactions with our surrounding environments, and are nourished by the ground we inhabit. We find signs of the Holy Spirit's presence in experiences of intense gratification—encounters in life that arouse in us profound, visceral religious responses. We see the signs in moments of wide-eyed discovery and jaw-dropping amazement, quiet relaxing of tension, energetic immersion in a project, spontaneous smiles, and that unmistakable look of someone whose motivations have changed. More importantly, since these experiences and responses tend to be so fleeting, we can listen for signs of the Spirit in people's stories—and we can remember and treasure such moments in our own histories.

But what of negative experiences? How do we find fruit in experiences that spawn intense fear and anxiety, a sense of enraging and shaming betrayal, a deadening loneliness, or prolonged boredom and *ennui*? Such experiences can drive people toward or away from God, depending on what they heed in themselves, what they hear and experience from others around them, and whether anyone notices their distress. Our emotions can serve as the deep, wordless language of the Holy Spirit's communication within us and with others, signaling us that something is terribly wrong. With God's help, we may be able to listen to the promptings in ourselves and from others to find the grace of such responses to awaken and stir us to defend ourselves, call for restoration of what is right, cherish whatever moments we can find with others, and look for purpose. And in our moments of desolation, we hope for fellow travelers who will see us wounded by the side of the road and help carry us to places of safety and healing. No pilgrim is guaranteed absolute safety—but fruit is born even in distress.

When people allow themselves the freedom to bear fruit, their actions and words cannot help but be evangelistic. By our natures, we are made to proclaim good news to one another and to all creation—and by doing so, we offer our sacrifice of gratitude to God and are enfolded in the good news of eternity. Take, for example, the story of a teenage soldier on duty who encountered a beggar without clothes, shivering in the cold. He took his cloak and divided it in two pieces, sharing the surplus of his warmth with the beggar. Later, after seeing Christ in a dream wearing half his cloak, he recognized his act as God's movement within him, and he immediately devoted his life to the service of Christ. This young soldier was Martin of Tours, fourth-century bishop and saint. As a young, uncertain pilgrim considering Christianity, at the prompting of his companion the Holy Spirit, he engaged in evangelistic action that resulted in his own transformation.

> [What] enabled people to come right into the kingdom depended so much on a chain of witnesses who had helped people through various stages of belief to come to the point where they were ready to make that final, decisive leap. — *Geoff Pearson*

But let's be clear: naming, recognizing, and celebrating the presence of God in people's lives and our own lives is not a simplistic game of "affirmations." We are not aiming to be like Al Franken's famously annoying *Saturday Night Live* character by saying to people, "You're good enough, you're smart enough, and doggone it, people like you." Our commitment "to seek and serve Christ in all persons"—to listen for, name, and celebrate the presence of the Holy Spirit in people's lives—means that we may need to help people dig deeply to find the Holy. This act of digging is a clearing away of debris—helping people move stuff out of the way that is blocking the hidden treasure. Good news may need to come in the form of a "hard word." You or I might need to ask a question like "What are you doing?" The direct question seems to be God's favored mode of confrontation: "Adam, where are you?" "Saul, Saul, why are you persecuting me?" When we ask people "What are you doing?" we invite them to pay attention to the same questions that have been in their own hearts, no matter how well suppressed. A confronting question, especially when said directly but without scorn, animosity, or pity, tells the other person two things: 1) "I see you and don't understand"; and 2) "I trust you to tell me your story honestly." In a different moment, when someone sees the consequences of his own decisions and actions unravel before him, we can ask a different kind of question: "How can we move on from here?"

---

evangelism as spiritual discipline

As you might already recognize from what I have written, I am absolutely convinced that evangelism cannot be scripted, programmed, or presented as a disembodied "word from on High." This means that one cannot simply flip on the "evangelism switch." Good news emerges; it cannot be forced. When I have been to a truly wonderful restaurant (anything from sushi to a barbecue joint to Chicago-style pizza to a French bistro), I do not have to script or force my enthusiasm. It just comes out naturally: "There's a great place you have *got* to try." And then I begin to tell the story, reliving the enjoyment I experienced at that particular restaurant.

No program or formula will work. Evangelism that emerges from our gratitude and compels us to speak is a *chosen* habit, a spiritual discipline of staying rooted in our gratitude. As witnesses to the love of God, we need three spiritual practices:

- ◆ I will remember my own wonder, joy, and gratitude.
- ◆ I will speak; I will tell my stories.
- ◆ I will meet other people listening for the Holy in their lives.

The most that a program can do is help us learn how to embrace these disciplines of mind and heart. But programs will not do the evangelism for us, or even make us better disciples. A discipline involves personal choice and commitment.

Emergent evangelism happens in the give-and-take of our everyday conversations and actions with others—and it is not a one-way experience. Because the sharing of good news depends on exchange with someone, we engage in evangelism by listening as well as (and probably more than) speaking. We who are listening for good news become the ones being evangelized.

Every year, I give my students an assignment that challenges them—an assignment of "evangelistic listening." Students go out in the city, find someone they don't know, and in one-on-one conversations ask these strangers about their beliefs, their deepest values, and their most profound life experiences. At every seminary where I have taught, students initially balk or have minor anxiety attacks. Many have never talked to strangers about matters of faith. Even though my sample questions do not directly mention God, students become anxious about "getting public" with something that they feel is too private or risky. But students inevitably return from this assignment stretched and transformed. They learn how to listen more deeply to and explore more freely for signs of the Spirit in everyday interactions with people they do not know. They learn that people are not as private or resistant as they thought to sharing their beliefs and values. They learn that it is not difficult to invite people to talk about things they usually don't get to talk about with other people.

When we finally embrace the freedom of this spiritual practice of bearing and speaking good news, then the church will grow freely from new soil and be transformed where it already stands. We will be more like the early Christians, who were

* passionate about Jesus;
* flexible in translating the gospel to meet people where they were;

- open to the Holy Spirit's transformation in their lives;
- committing themselves to the living God;
- willing to go anywhere people gathered— including their own homes; and
- engaging in personal conversations regularly with others.[17]

You may wonder why I have focused so much on evangelism that is based in gratitude, wonder, joy, and delight. After reading multiple books on evangelism and listening to any number of speeches and sermons, I came to the conclusion that something crucial was missing. Too often I hear evangelism linked with duty, a kind of Christian obligation, something in the fine print that wasn't told to us when we first became Christians but that we must take on as our responsibility or deal with significant guilt. Too often, I hear evangelism linked with a negative urgency to rescue people from their depravity, to help people recognize their lowly estate and desperate circumstances, so that they will turn to Christ out of fear of damnation. These may or may not be ultimately legitimate motivations for evangelism—but the fact that so many church leaders seem to resort to the language of duty or fear suggests to me that they are not really entirely convinced that God's love has sufficient power in the end of itself to transform lives. Perhaps they do not believe that God really desires us, but only that God is grudgingly doing us a favor. Perhaps they do not believe that love can truly motivate a person with any sense of urgency, and that we will only in our depravity—even as redeemed Christians—seek and cling to God's love for ourselves.

The thinking of some evangelists is along these lines: psychologically, people will not respond to God's relentless love unless they realize how far they are removed from it and how little they deserve it. People only turn to God for one selfish reason: the rescue of their souls from eternal

Love is enough!

damnation. Thus, people only seek God because guilt and fear have been aroused, and they want relief from the burden of these feelings. Such evangelism relies on manipulation of human emotion through an arousal of needy desperation—because love alone is not enough to turn the human heart.

Obviously, I do not share these low opinions of God and humanity. But...is there a similar urgency to gratitude and joy? Does gratitude for God's goodness generate enough energy to propel us out to a waiting universe? Do joy and wonder at the vastness of God's love for us really energize us and generate within us the fruits of the Spirit? Ebullience can be a strong motivation—but does it have the same pressing urgency as the determination to save souls from darkness and damnation? I once heard a church planter tell me that without a vivid belief in hell and eternal damnation, one would not find the driving energy necessary to be a truly successful evangelist. Is the threat of punishment really a more powerful or fundamental motivation than joyful and awed gratitude for love?

> The one who evangelizes is a witness and not a judge. — *David Bosch*

What does a focus on fear and guilt get us? At best, yes, a few people will respond with horrified recognition of their own sins and errors in life—their own willful wandering—and a deep sense of gratitude and relief at God's pardon. But the language of judgment and condemnation—a language not given to us but with which only Christ is charged—divides, separates, and arouses people's shame, anger, and resistance. Aggressive confrontation immediately divides you from the other, sets up perceptions of superiority and inferiority, and touches a host of inner voices that either wallow in self-loathing or resist any kind of condemnation. Any professionals working with people know that direct manipulation of fear and guilt can only rarely be used as primary means of motivating people, and then with uncertain and not necessarily enduring results.

The ebullience of gratitude and wonder creates an intense—and remarkably different—kind of urgency. It is the kind of urgency that makes us blurt out good news to people we know, and even people we don't know. It is the urgency of laughter. Bursting out from the inside, it is as if we find ourselves saying, "I can't withhold telling you my joy, because it is so urgent, it is so remarkable." In the grip of vitalizing gratitude, we are propelled beyond ourselves to tell others our good news. The Samaritan woman abandons her water jar, runs back to the city, and says, "Come and see a man who told me everything I have ever done! He cannot be the Messiah, can he?" (John 4:29). Note that it is not the certainty of her doctrinal claims, but the heartfelt intensity of her testimony that brings people to believe in Jesus. Jesus' followers together were taken up in joy shouting "Hosanna" and waving palms when he entered Jerusalem—and Jesus, knowing joy's power, knew that to restrain them would mean that the joy would have to leak out somewhere, even from the rocks. The pair on the road to Emmaus found their hearts burning within them when they met and listened to the Jesus they did not recognize—and their joy propelled them that night back to Jerusalem to tell the other disciples what they had seen.

Bishop Ting of China has for many years recognized the pitfalls of any theology that limits or subjugates the boundless nature of the God who is Love. He started with a fundamental question: How can the message of fallen humanity, sin, and Christ's rescue from sin be maintained in Chinese culture, where such a dark view of humanity is not assumed or taken for granted? Bishop Ting found in God's love the central theme that for him resonated with the deepest spiritual yearnings and motivations of the

Chinese people—belonging, wholeness, harmony, and connection. His theology begins with this statement from *Love Never Ends:* "The root attribute of God is not his omnipotence, or his omniscience, or his omnipresence, or his self-existence, or his majesty and glory, but his love." Focusing on God's love led Ting back to the deep core values in his own culture—and he seeks and celebrates signs of this God-given love in his people, whether Christian or non-Christian. While still acknowledging the reality of sin and human frailty, Ting places primary emphasis on seeing the image of God in people and trusts that the Holy Spirit inhabits all the world. For Ting, evangelism begins with the assumption that "both Christians and non-Christians have been created in the image of God. The world in which the Holy Spirit dwells is one world."[18]

What is evoked psychologically by an urgency of delight, wonder, gratitude, and joy? To be held in the grip of gratitude is one of the fundamental human hungers. The gratitude of others for what we are and what we offer is also a fundamental human hunger. Shame and angry resistance cannot long endure the gaze of loving delight, but will begin to evaporate. I want to be recognized for what I truly am, despite my failures and other people's assumptions. I want to hear and receive the word, "I honor you," and "You are my delight." I want to be delighted in, to be named, to be known with joy and wonder at my being. I want my life to be seen as a bit of evidence of God's presence and work in the world—perhaps broken and missing the mark, but nonetheless surrounded and infused by Love.

How many people are desperate for such an experience of loving delight and gratitude for their being? How many may not know how to receive such a gift because they cannot recall ever having received such a gift? Here we come to the real desperation of the sinner and the sinned-against. The deeper and more enduring the wounds we inflict and have inflicted upon us, the more we doubt the possibility of boundless love taking us, and the more we give up hope of finding ourselves in the grip of gratitude. I remember testing a young boy for learning disabilities during my psychology training. After terrible abuse by his father and mother, he had gone in rapid succession through three foster homes—a behavioral terror himself. In a room alone with me, the boy became incredibly agitated, repeatedly ran to various places in the room to find things he could hit me with, and took hold of my tie in an attempt to choke me. He had no control of his aggression—once fear had taken hold, almost automatically, he descended into pure fight-or-flight responding. Here was a boy for whom "love" was a concept it would take years to experience, trust, and name—and the dedication needed by others in word and action to begin to undo the damage was enormous.

All around us is a hungry, hungry world, waiting with cries and groans for the Love it does not realize already accompanies it, suffers with it, calls it to new life. Our joy stands ready to respond. But it takes courage to offer the good news of God's love in our actions and words, to tell our own stories of wonder and gratitude. It takes courage to believe in resurrection and Love's final triumph.

The good news is God's passionate pursuit of us. There is no place too dark, empty, tragic, or broken—or too noble, self-sufficient, or bright—for God to go before us and follow us, luring and beckoning us to new and fuller life. Jesus is for us the core experience of God's persistent love for humanity—the deliverer who dares to offer God's love in the face of all rejection, betrayal, and destruction, who triumphs over our worst intentions and actions. In Jesus Christ, we know that God will go to any length to bring us into the transforming embrace of Love. This is the good news running beneath all of the stories we tell—

not only the Great Stories at the core of our Christian faith, but our own stories as well, and the stories of those to whom we listen.

---

why does God need evangelists?

Unfortunately, *laissez-faire* thinking is common in the church. Good Christian parents, clergy, and faith communities have for a few generations practiced benign neglect, claiming that they do not want to impose Christian faith, values, or ideals on their children because they want to allow their children's spiritual life to emerge and grow freely—and anyway, the mere experience of spiritual education by osmosis (in worship, occasional hearing of scripture, and being around "good people") is sufficient for our children who are such natural sponges. Good Christian citizens have also practiced benign neglect of people in need, claiming that aid and assistance breed dependency, that "God helps those who help themselves" (a statement often quoted as from the Bible, but one that is actually from Benjamin Franklin). Why do we need Christian educators? Why do we need to be spiritual advocates? Shouldn't we let people find and exercise their own God-given powers and motivations to search for and find love, truth, and justice?

Why does God need evangelists? If evangelism begins and ends with the Holy Spirit, if the good news is God's passionate love of all humanity, and if conversion is the work of God in deep conversation with each person, family, or community, then why does God need us as evangelists?

Simply put, as human beings we have difficulty knowing or remembering who we are. Without someone to name us, we can forget who we are. The sociological concept of the "Looking-Glass Self" suggests that we only come to know ourselves and to develop a sense of identity from what others reflect back to us—from what we witness as our impact on others. A similar concept has found its way into some strands of contemporary psychotherapy: "mirroring." A healthy and whole self develops in relationship with others who act as mirrors to us, showing to us and naming for us what we have just showed them. It begins simply with mothers and fathers echoing, mimicking, and expanding on their infants' actions and emotional expressions. It continues through childhood, adolescence, and all our adult lives with parents, elders, counselors, mentors, and confidantes who hear us and respond to our heartfelt expressions in kind.

Preventing the Pollyanna Effect

Many of us have encountered what we might call "smiley Christians." They smile a lot more than seems natural. They seem to coo or croon rather than talk. They have adopted a seemingly foreign language with phrases that sound artificial. Yes, it is possible to slip into artifice and fake joy, but there are some fundamental differences between a "Pollyanna approach" and a deeply grounded spiritual practice of lived and spoken gratitude.

First, it is possible for someone to offer a practiced performance of fake joy and not really be present. Telling your own stories and listening for others' stories of encounters with God the Lover of humanity requires your own words, your own language, your own genuine experience of gratitude.

Second, we do not always need to be happy to recount our stories of gratitude and wonder. The Psalms are full of examples of individuals in great distress who nonetheless recall times of redemption and release, for them and for their people.

Third, and most important, when we really begin with listening, we will hear real stories of toxicity and harm in the church. In these moments, smiles and platitudes have no place. We must continue to listen, be prepared to offer our deepest sorrow and confession on behalf of the church, name and honor the anger and grief as God-given, and wait to hear the stories of gratitude and wonder that people have encountered elsewhere.

With the recent discovery of what researchers are calling "mirror neurons," it looks like we are hardwired for mirroring others and responding to being mirrored. We come to know ourselves and remember who we are because we are known and named. Without honest, free, and consistent mirroring, we can lose our bearings and become confused about who we are. Implied in both these concepts is a responsibility incumbent upon people to act as mirrors to one another—to reflect back what they receive. We help create one another.

In the spiritual practice of evangelism, we are really engaging in helping people see their true identity, and reminding ourselves of our true identity. When we name God's presence, we reflect back to others what we see as something deeply true about their being. Without this mirroring, people run the risk of forgetting who they really are in the eyes of God. But when we are really fully engaged with another person we find the courage to name what we see of her soul. It is through us that the gospel holds up its unique mirror to the reality of each person's life.

for whom are we evangelists?

There are so many people in so many places who do not know the name of their joy or wonder. Where do we begin?

Let us begin with our households. Our gratitude and wonder can first propel us toward our own families. Indeed, they are our first responsibility. To neglect our children on matters of faith is to refuse them the language with which to name God's presence and movement in their lives. To remain silent with our grandchildren, nieces, and nephews about God's love, out of some misplaced respect for the privacy of the nuclear family, is to deprive them of images and stories that can shape their lives. To rely on the institution of the church for giving our children religion, but not to discuss matters of church and of daily faith and life throughout the week, teaches our children to disconnect religion from the rest of life rather than allow Christianity to become a way of life.

Sarah, a colleague of mine in graduate school, went to India to study the ways Hindu beliefs were taught to children in Maharashtra. She found one of the most evocative practices I have ever heard. In Maharashtrian villages, the women take white chalky paint and create on the reddish walls of their homes images of the gods and of the great Hindu stories. From time to time they change the pictures, washing the walls and creating new images. The household is immersed in sacred stories, and the children grow up with images and stories surrounding them in their most intimate and familiar environment.

Hear, O Israel: The LORD is our God, the LORD alone. You shall love the LORD your God with all your heart, and with all your soul, and with all your might. Keep these words that I am commanding you today in your heart. Recite them to your children and talk about them when you are at home and when you are away, when you lie down and when you rise. *(Deuteronomy 6:4–7)*

I remembered Sarah's story when we were expecting our first daughter, Cassie. I asked an artist from the church I was serving to come and paint some murals on the walls of our baby's bedroom, depicting the seven days of creation. For the first year after Cassie was born, until we moved and left our house, every night before putting her to bed we carried her around her room to each mural and told her each part of the story. From her earliest age, we talked to her about what we were doing during church services; we prayed with her; we told her Bible stories; and we told her how much God loves her.

Immersing our households with stories of God and our experiences of love is not an impossible task. It simply

involves a shift in habit—an opening of our everyday speech and actions to include space for the gratitude and wonder and delight that come from being loved by the Creator. This is evangelism at home—expressing our gratitude for love, naming the Source of that love, telling our stories of God's goodness, and talking clearly and honestly about the choices we make, for good and for ill. We need not wait for our children to ask us why we do things the way we do; we can ask them, like Jesus asked his disciples after he washed their feet, "Do you know why I have done this?" When we think and talk with our children, we have the opportunity to help them—and ourselves—see how deeply connected our conduct is with our stories. Our Christian values and beliefs are rooted in our individual and shared stories, as parts of the "Great Narrative" of redemption.

We as children and grandchildren are also evangelists in our families—to our siblings, parents, grandparents, aunts, and uncles. When God awakens us, stirs our imaginations, or fills our hearts, we cannot help but share good news with those we love. Children, youth, young adults, and young parents are often powerful witnesses to God the Lover of humanity. We speak of Jesus and of God's presence in our lives with an incisive clarity and power—in our doubts as well as our convictions. Our homes become a place of holy encounter because we seek, yearn, mourn, and celebrate with a directness that recalls for our elders their own days of searching and of finding.

The home becomes even more powerful as a place of divine encounter when we open them to fellow pilgrims. As Christians, we serve as evangelists to one another, sharing in the deep spiritual practice of listening to and telling our stories of joy and wonder and lament, and of naming the presence of the God who is our companion on our pilgrimages. In home fellowship, we learn how to practice the evangelism that emerges from love.

We not only welcome fellow Christian pilgrims. In each others' homes, we enter a new space of familiarity with our friends, neighbors, and colleagues. We hear stories of pilgrimage. We are given opportunities to listen for the footsteps of the Holy Spirit in others' lives, and to offer our own wondrous stories.

This kind of evangelism responds to the tribal impulses of youth, young adults, and, truth be known, adults of all ages. We all seek to find and create our "tribes" of people with whom we connect around passions and yearnings. Out of these new bonds, relationships, and networks, community is born anew. Our neighborhoods, schools, parks, and stores can all become places into which we bring our acts and words propelled by Love. In the natural exchanges with other parents in playgroups, teammates or companions in sports and exercise, and shop owners and wait staff at stores and restaurants we frequent, we have opportunities to tell others who we are and to hear and celebrate their stories. We become participants in the Holy Spirit's work of knitting together human community.

In most parts of the world where there is an explosion of Christianity these days, home meetings are critical to the growth. — *Michael Green*

At the parish I served in Evanston, Illinois, a young professional woman, Marie, who had taken time to be at home with her young children, began to talk with other young mothers about the challenges of giving up a career to be a stay-at-home mom. Discussions of faith, Christian life, and church experience naturally came up in her conversations. Soon, there was a group of young families attending St. Mark's and hosting a midweek playgroup for toddlers and their stay-at-home parents. Marie started to walk the neighborhood around the church with her stroller, talking to parents she met about this experience of joy at St. Mark's. This struck some church staff and regular members as a bit "out there," but the new life and energy she and others brought to the church was welcomed and celebrated.

The lure of the Holy Spirit, the ebullience of gratitude, does not restrict us merely to those most like us or to the people who live in our own neighborhoods. Love propels us ever outward, pressing against our own self-imposed and culturally defined habits. Let us dare to go to people who are not like us. Whether we speak of class, race, level of education, political persuasion, health, age, sexuality, or marital status, we live with a constant awareness of divisions between us and categories by which we define one another. Evangelism propelled by Love draws us across these divisions. Our experiences of gratitude, wonder, delight, and joy at God's work in our lives do not have a limited audience, nor is the Holy Spirit's activity limited in scope. Our public work for the common good—in community organizing and political efforts, in social service, in partnerships across racial dividing lines—brings us into contact with people with whom we might otherwise have little in common. Our careers bring us into contact with students, patients, customers, and clients who live very different lives from our own. Our interactions and exchanges with people on buses, airplanes, subways, and the street bring us face to face with Christ the stranger who has become a fellow sojourner. As much as we are able and willing, as much as we allow ourselves to be freed by joy and propelled by gratitude, we have opportunities to carry our sacred stories and our words and acts of love into our relationships with people unlike us (and yet not so unlike us)—conservative to liberal, gay to straight, robust to frail, old to young, black to Asian, Latino to white. When we are propelled by Love, we do not know where we will be led in our evangelistic pilgrimage. It is a great adventure.

But as we cross into new places, we are faced with the challenge of learning new languages and ways of expression. How we speak matters. How then shall we speak? How do we tell our stories to people who have never heard them?

Religious language can become "jargon" that is off-putting to those who don't speak it. Words that we use freely in the church mean something to us, but they usually do not translate into anything meaningful for outsiders, and they may even conjure up unhelpful images or associations. One such word is "salvation." Earlier we noted the cultural shift in the United States away from concern with salvation or eternal life—particularly among young adults. We should *not* take this as some sign of our society's abandonment of God, but we *can* recognize that our culture has shifted focus spiritually—and become more attuned to what has changed and what speaks most elementally of the riches of God's good news.

The word "salvation" itself is rooted in ancient Roman culture. *Salvé*, or "good health," was a common public greeting, related directly to the modern French *salut*. The public greeting conveyed something of the meaning of "salvation"—a solution from beyond one's own efforts to address deep needs. It was not far from "good luck" or "good fate" in its connotations. In a world in which fates and gods and demigods and all sorts of external forces were acting upon people, it was natural to hope for *salve*—the good fortune of good health and well-being.

But the word did not resonate in the same ways with new and changing cultures. In other cultures and times salvation has meant victory over evil, liberation, reconciliation, or redemption of suffering. During the Industrial Revolution, John Wesley and other Methodist preachers shifted focus, making use of one of the elemental meanings of the word "salvation"—"good health"—by focusing on healing. This had powerful resonance with Americans dealing with the onslaught of the industrialization and its impact on health—physical, mental, familial, and social. Similarly, liberation theologian Gustavo Gutiérrez, Archbishop Oscar Romero, and other church leaders in Central America found eager recipients of the good news of salvation as Christ setting all people free from the bonds of oppression.

As we have seen, Bishop Ting recognized that "salvation" had a different meaning for Chinese people and searched for new language to connect the gospel story with their concerns, passions, and fundamental assumptions. He worked his way back to the elemental concept of love. Ting found the Holy in the midst of a socialist society and government that few Western Christians were willing to acknowledge as anything but evil—because he took the time to listen to the hearts and deep desires of his fellow Chinese citizens. Ting gave socialism a theological name: "Love organized for the masses of the people."[19] His wife, Siu May Ting, has been quoted as saying, "As Chinese Christians we do not see Christianity and socialist China as opposed to each other. It is God working, whether in his name or not."[20]

For us to find ways to share our beliefs, values, and stories with others creatively, we must immerse ourselves in the cultural and personal realities to which we bring good news. As we listen deeply to people, we will find that new words and concepts present themselves to help us name the Holy in our lives and share our sacred stories. More subtly, a profound crossing between us and others will develop as we share personal stories of gratitude and wonder. Eventually our own language of faith will expand.

Three of Jesus' parables can help us orient ourselves for the practice of evangelism. First, in the parable of the sower and the seeds (Matthew 13:3–9), Jesus calls us to orient ourselves toward *boundless and unjudging generosity*. This parable is not simply about sorting out good ground from bad, or the determination of who is in or out. This parable more significantly begins with the absolutely careless, profligate love of God—revealed *and practiced* in the work of the sower. The parable describes the unjudging generosity and optimism of the evangelist: his visionary hope that all ground will blossom, his trust in God's Spirit that is the source of life for all seeds, and his expectation simply to sow freely. Missioners and church planters have described this as an "unleashed" approach to ministry and evangelism. Such an approach does not run contrary to Episcopal theology, even if it does fly in the face of Episcopal institutional polity and love of "good order." Regardless of where our pilgrimage takes us, our stance is to be that of the sower practicing disorderly and wasteful agriculture. Wherever we journey, we spread the seed of the good news of God's love, without daring to make some judgment about whether or not our children, parents, friends, neighbors, colleagues, and other fellow travelers will be receptive.

Second, in the parable of the talents (Matthew 25:14–30), Jesus helps us see that evangelism born of gratitude is freely public. Jesus orients us toward a habit of *free public exchange of the gifts of the kingdom,* unhindered by personal or corporate shame, anxiety, or biases. The parable of the talents helps us understand that kingdom life, even possibly redemption itself, depends on real sharing in the wide public sphere what God has given us to share. Whatever God has given us are gifts and talents for us to use, to bring out and display in public, to offer with unabashed eagerness and shrewdness. Our generosity with the gifts of God, which we share and trade liberally in our communities, will never return to us empty. God's love propels us to action—or else that love never reaches fulfillment.

The greatest barrier to the free and public use of God's gifts is our own private anxieties and biases. But none of the servants in the parable complained they lost their shirts for publicly trading their talents, nor about ending up with a net loss in the marketplace. In God's economy, talents and gifts multiply as they are publicly exchanged. The only loss is in a retreat from God's invitation to wield our talents as instruments that convey God's generosity.

If we recognize that God's gifts are meant to be public, if we take God's generosity of love to heart and allow it to propel us outward, and if we enter our many public worlds with an expectation that in each encounter we will meet Christ and have the opportunity to receive gifts as well as give them, we will find our little anxieties and biases receding into the background as we are taken up into a new way of being with others.

> We intend to uphold and uplift love and will propagate this loving spirit amongst people. To let love, the love of Christ, awaken the many frozen hearts of the society.
> — K. H. Ting, God is Love

Third, as found in the parables of the good shepherd (Luke 15:3–7 and John 10:7–16), Jesus orients us toward *God's preference for those who are lost or at risk.* God's agrarian accounting is focused not on who is present in the fold, but who is missing. Christ seeks those who to the rest of the flock appear lost. Christ calls them—and they know and respond to Christ's voice. Christ returns with the wandering sheep, and calls for a celebration.

Jesus' extensive interest in those outside the fold expands to encompass many communities as yet unknown to us: "I have other sheep that do not belong to this fold" (John 10:16). Such a shift in our interest to those outside the fold will lead us into interactions with people whose experiences of God and the world are different from our own because of social class, racial and cultural background, educational experiences, and religion. Evangelism begins with listening for the work of God in other people's lives in new contexts that stretch our culturally constrained imaginations. As Jesus himself experienced with the Samaritan woman, the centurion soldier, the Canaanite woman, and the Gerazene demoniac, God's interest is in all humanity. We ourselves are transformed by encounters with those who are "not like us."

This was precisely the experience of social and evangelistic missionaries such as Cyril and Methodius in the ninth century, who learned the Slavic language of the Khazar region and created a new "Glagolithic" alphabet (which has over centuries been modified and adapted into contemporary Cyrillic) to translate Christian scriptures and liturgies into Slavic. Against constant pressure from other church officials who for the sake of uniformity demanded that the Slavs hear scripture and liturgy in Latin, they defended the rights of Slavic Christians of Khazar to hear scripture and celebrate the liturgy in their own languages. Early in the twentieth century a woman named Annie Farthing left Illinois in the early 1900s to work for the Episcopal mission projects in Alaska. Beginning her work among prospectors, wanderers, and laborers of all races at St. Matthew's Hospital in Fairbanks, she discovered a deep love for the native peoples of Alaska. Mission leaders gave her charge of a new mission in Nenana, where she led a school. She died shortly thereafter, defending a young girl from the advances of an abusive alcoholic wanderer.

In the second half of the twentieth century, attorney William Stringfellow dedicated his career to direct social advocacy and providing free legal aid in Harlem in New York City. He moved into a tenement slum in Harlem to practice what he saw in the gospels as Jesus' own habit of "pitching tent" among all humans—and he won the trust of many who had grown suspicious of well-meaning but socially detached do-gooders. He was also sought after by law and business schools, where he helped students see the deeply ingrained and unquestioned systems that supported social and racial injustice. In this century Marla Ruzicka, who died at age twenty-eight from a roadside bomb in Iraq, had dedicated her entire young adult life to work with victims of AIDS, poverty, and war. She was known by weary and jaded aid workers in Iraq for her energy, devotion, and optimism, even as she worked with hundreds of civilians who had lost loved ones and property.

> To have a job where you can make things better for people? That's a blessing. Why would I do anything else?
> — Marla Ruzicka, speaking to a San Francisco reporter

Each of these evangelists found passionate and unrelenting love for the people to whom they felt God leading them. This love was neither superior nor apologetic in tone—it was a love that propelled them by the prophetic vision of God's embrace of all humanity, a love that grew as they met the profound presence of the Holy Spirit in the lives of people who were different from them.

Michael, one of my seminary students, found himself a few years ago as an unlikely but happy evangelist. He went with a friend from his church to a biker bar in the working-class city of Antioch, California. When he saw all the men and women dressed in leather and denim, he wondered to himself, "What am I getting myself into?" but he sat down and began a conversation with a group of bikers. Soon, with the help of some religious images in commercials on the big-screen TV, Michael gradually turned the topic of conversation to religion and faith. Over the next several hours, he found himself surrounded by twelve bikers who had lots of questions and were eager for answers. After about four hours of intense conversation, one of the men asked, "So, what do we need to do to be baptized?" Michael, not wanting to lose the moment of opportunity, led them in prayers, baptized them, and welcomed twelve new Christians into the household of God. One the bikers joked, "Well, still, if I set foot in a church, lightning will strike." Michael invited them all to come to his church, largely filled with retired and wealthy suburbanites. One month later, the bikers all showed up at the church—to be welcomed heartily by Michael and the congregation, which responded warmly to them. The moment we dare to step out on the path of evangelistic pilgrimage—the journey of "white martyrdom" taken by our Celtic ancestors—is the moment we open ourselves, and the church, to surprising transformation. We will find ourselves face to face with people we never would have thought to call brother or sister, hearing and speaking Christ to one another.

In 1997 I had the pleasure of meeting Bill, a curate in the rather moribund parish of Huntingdon, England, in the diocese of Ely. Bill took the challenge of evangelism seriously. Besides serving as a chaplain to the "biker" community in eastern England, he became a friend and confidante of a group of young men and women who, through needle-sharing, had all contracted HIV together. They had begun to develop some early AIDS symptoms—but they stayed together and committed themselves to one another and to each other's care for the rest of their lives, however long that was going to be. They met on a regular basis in a bar with Bill. He told me, "I see in this community a greater sense of Christ-like love for one another than I have seen in my own church. They did this thing of sharing needles not as a way of saving money, but as a way of sharing brotherhood and sisterhood. They were initially seeking a type of communion—blood fellowship—and unfortunately through that action, they dealt each other death. But what they were seeking is deeply profound. I hope that before we begin to lose some of them, we can gather some of them at the table for true fellowship, the true Communion in the sharing of Christ's Body and Blood."

Bill offers a profound understanding how God's Spirit is at work among people many churches would not think to approach or touch. He offers a model of how to bridge the gulf between two worlds through a deep listening for the footsteps of the Holy Spirit. It takes a profound belief in Christ's seeking out the sheep who are not of his fold, a willingness to find new language to name the Holy and speak the good news, and a vigorous hope that these friends would find their home in Christ.

chapter three

Living the Pilgrim Faith
Models of Evangelism

 Neither the one who plants nor the one who waters is anything, but only God who gives the growth.
(1 Corinthians 3:7)

What does evangelism actually look like in the life of faithful Christians in the church? How does it work out in the day-to-day ministries of individuals and their communities of faith? How can congregations and dioceses support and develop people's practices of sharing God's good news with their families, colleagues, neighbors, and friends? What does it look like to approach the "stranger"?

Think of this chapter as a "travel guide" to places around the Episcopal Church where the seeds of transformation are being sown. It highlights places on the roadmap for the pilgrim evangelist in each of us. These stories present intentionally, vibrantly, and uniquely evangelistic ministries created by individuals and their faith communities to meet real hunger for the gospel. They include ministries and programs with children, youth, and families, programs with young adults, and new "church plants." The stories range across the United States, from east to west and south to north. They involve people of all ages, racial and ethnic backgrounds, and theological perspectives—in many settings, rural to urban, poor to wealthy.

As you read these stories, however, remember one important thing: they are not ultimately about that particular program or this particular parish. More important are the highly interpersonal practices of evangelism by individual members of these congregations and programs *in their daily lives.* The evangelistic success in each ministry is completely dependent on individuals who, having come together as fellow pilgrims and having learned a spirit of evangelism, carry good news out on their journeys into a waiting and hungry world, bearing grateful witness to God's transforming love.

new congregations in unfamiliar places: church plants

An obvious place to look in the Episcopal Church for practices of evangelism is among "church plants"—new mission congregations with a commitment to reaching people who have no faith or community or support. Three of these relatively new churches are thriving because individuals, existing congregations, and dioceses embarked on highly creative work and followed the Holy Spirit to give birth to these vibrant communities of faith.

NUESTRA SEÑORA DE GUADALUPE, WAUKEGAN, ILLINOIS

The fastest growing church in the Episcopal Diocese of Chicago in the early 2000s, the Latino mission Nuestra Señora de Guadalupe in Waukegan, Illinois, is also the strongest among Episcopal congregations involved in the expanding Latino communities of the metropolitan Chicago area. Waukegan's Latino community has grown rapidly to more than 40 percent of the city's population, bringing a new sense of fluidity and movement to this working-class city. Nuestra Señora's small original congregation had not found a way to reach the surrounding Latino community effectively, but with the leadership of Narciso Diaz and the vigorous partnership of Church of the Holy Spirit in Lake Forest, Illinois, discovered new energy for outreach and evangelism.

Christ Church in Waukegan and Church of the Holy Spirit in Lake Forest joined as a team with the diocese to support this new congregation. Holy Spirit provided housing for the vicar, Narciso Diaz, and Christ Church provided space for the congregation to meet. In less than a year, the congregation grew to a point that they had to move out of the chapel to the main church. The vicar focused his ministry in the surrounding community, visiting people's homes and having conversations with them, holding Bible studies and other meetings, explaining the Episcopal Church, and offering sacramental ministry.

By 2002, Nuestra Señora already had five hundred members. They restored a formerly closed Lutheran church that had been purchased for them by Church of the Holy Spirit. George Carey, the former Archbishop of Canterbury, concluded his ministry with a visit to Nuestra Señora and helped lead the service of church consecration. Currently, weekly attendance is around 450, with over 750 on Easter.

In 2005, Nuestra Señora received additional funding to hire an associate priest, Gary Cox, who had worked with Latino congregations in South America. Gary was surprised by two things at Nuestra Señora: the strength of relationships among members, and the strong attraction of sacramental ministries. "There are many family networks and friendships in the congregation. The whole relationship network is very much evident.... People tell each other that this is a church where they can participate, where people are friendly."

Because of their congregational partnership, members from Church of the Holy Spirit have been able to witness for themselves the significant outreach and ministry of Nuestra Señora. The leading liaison member, Bob Hernandez, shared the following story:

> One Sunday, we were having a partnership meeting at their church. I went into the nave, and there were all these children and mothers. I asked Rosa, "What's going on?" She looked at me strangely, and said, "This is Catechism instruction. We have ninety-four registered children." Ninety-four children! This is one of the most important things happening here. At least thirty children a year are confirmed.

Bob has been particularly moved by the intense devotion and mutual affection emerging from Nuestra Señora. "I ask, 'Why do you come to this church?' They say, 'We went to the Catholic church or other churches—we showed up a little before and left a little after and never came back until the next week. Now, we are all here and it is *our* church, and we are doing things all week—children and adult education, retreats for men, women, and couples, the Order of Mary, and a lot of social activities.'" Bob described how people show their gratitude for the love of Christ encountered through Nuestra Señora. For instance, Antonio, a roofer, "brought his roofing team to work on the church. He'd get out of his truck, wouldn't say a word, and his workers would get out the shingles and repair the roof. He's been gone for a year, back in Mexico—but gives a pledge."

Bob has found his own life changed by his involvement in this shared ministry, as the stories he hears at Nuestra Señora connect with stories in his own life.

Narciso told a story of a woman whose boyfriend did not attend church. She brought him to church. He had never received the sacrament. Narciso worked with him—he has been baptized, has had his first communion, and they are now married. There are other stories like that—frequently the woman or wife bringing the man she lives with. Sometimes, it's the man. The senior warden, one of the original twelve, brought his wife and family. That's some of my story, too. I was raised Catholic, but my first wife was Jewish. So, after high school I stopped going. My second wife asked me to come occasionally to Holy Spirit at Lake Forest beginning with Easter, and then a few times, and then every week. Now I am deeply involved—teaching Sunday school and confirmation, working on stewardship, taking part in the search committee for a new priest. Now that I'm retired, I have as much time as I want to devote to the church.

Waukegan is a working-class city. Along with families facing challenges of making ends meet, the city has faced an increase in gangs and gang-related crime. "Padre Diaz" quickly recognized these challenges and made them an integral part of the evangelistic ministry of Nuestra Señora. He worked on developing personal relationships with youth and families in the community, helping people navigate the challenges of immigration and consistently offering Bible study in different parishioners' homes. He has reached out to Latino gang leaders specifically, inviting them to church for Bible study and reflection and attending their school games. He has also worked with the parents of gang members, to help them redevelop systems of support and influence in their children's lives.

Narciso also expects his congregation to help in the evangelistic effort, and fosters partnerships with other organizations involved in spiritual outreach to the Latino community. When he first came to the parish, he asked two or three couples in that original group to invite others to their homes and studied the Bible with them. They heard the gospel, and became curious about the church. Attendance started growing very rapidly—thirty-five, then fifty, then one hundred and beyond. When the Bible studies grew too big for people's homes, they started meeting at church. Now the whole congregation is making a difference in the lives of their friends, families, and neighbors. They feed people regularly from their parking lot and hope to establish both a community daycare center and a labor center to help connect people with potential employers. Narciso's preaching has reflected the passion of the members of this community, with a call to follow Christ, to raise their heads and be proud, and to offer the goods of their hearts to one another.

> What is attractive is that Narciso is accessible, a listener, and willing to accompany them on their spiritual journey, as well as to accompany them on their daily journey.... And then, he is surrounded by a community of members who were there when the mission was formed, who love one another.
> —Bishop Scantlebury, Diocese of Chicago

Nuestra Señora is thriving, thanks in no small part to the unique and visionary partnership with Church of the Holy Spirit in Lake Forest. Holy Spirit members have contributed nearly $700,000 as well as their personal investments of time and talents since they dedicated themselves in 2000 to helping Nuestra Señora develop the strongest evangelistic ministry it could. This outpouring of generosity came as a natural outgrowth of Holy Spirit's spiritual pilgrimage: The congregation committed itself at a deeper level, for many years, to spiritual growth, which it describes on its website as "a deepening of our relation-ship with God, which we discover as we follow Jesus, guided by the Holy Spirit." Holy Spirit continues to be of great support to Narciso and to the whole congregation, and periodically they join together for celebrations, events, and worship. It is a ministry of evangelism that goes both ways. People of Holy Spirit are learning Spanish while people at Waukegan learn English, and a spirit of evangelism has infected both congregations as they talk with each other and share their stories. Coming to know one another through their shared mission, members of both congregations have experienced moments of profound wonder and gratitude, as they recognize Christ—and themselves—in one another.

From the beginning of Holy Spirit's involvement, the rector George Councell told his congregation that this partnership relied on building and maintaining relationships: "You need to see Christ in every person in front of you." Bob Hernandez says, "George worried me because he treated me as a more capable person than I really am." Bob became one of the key people in building relationships and bearing stories from one congregation to another. "Now, I can't imagine not being involved in working with Nuestra Señora. When I was first thinking and praying about all this, I thought, when I settle my final accounts, of God asking me, 'Bob, I gave you every opportunity and put all these things together. Why didn't you help make this happen?' And I couldn't stand the thought of that."

But Bob traces the success of the entire evangelistic effort back to the original members of Nuestra Señora. "Although everybody says that things would not have happened without me, I would not be standing in front of the church telling this story if those twelve to sixteen people at Nuestra Señora had not asked for a full-time priest. There were so many things that came together to make this happen. Yes, I am the voice-piece, and the one who tells the story—but it all depends on the generosity of everyone, including Narciso, those twelve original members, the diocese, and the people of Holy Spirit."

ST. NICHOLAS' CHURCH, KAPOLEI, HAWAII

St. Nicholas' Church in Kapolei, Hawaii, is a new congregation—filled with new Christians. After only three years, St. Nicholas' grew to 150 members strong, with about seventy to one hundred attending each week (120 on strong Sundays, and about 250 on Easter). Their community is very diverse, including Filipino, Caucasian, Hawaiian, Japanese, Latino, and African-American members, across a range of social class and education.

As their priest, Hollis Wright, told me, "The majority of our folks had little or no exposure to Christianity. This is all new to them. And we have folks that were raised as 'nominal' Christians, where the family attended church occasionally, but their life-decisions were not informed by faith."

Hollis accepted a call in 2003 to plant a new church in partnership with the twelve remaining members of the dying congregation of St. Barnabas' in Kapolei. Bishop Bob Fitzpatrick described the history of St. Barnabas as a "failed church-move" from Eva Beach to Kapolei in early 1990s, after decades of "hanging on" as a very small and struggling congregation. The bishop spent three years himself with them, guiding them through some self-study and decision-making, and at the end the remaining members agreed to close the church. Bob then worked on developing a spirit of evangelism with the remaining few, through a steady practice of Bible study and personal sharing. "It was an easy group to work with, because they were at rock-bottom, and if they didn't embrace some change and sense of mission, the place would not exist." The remaining twelve people began to view themselves and others differently, and committed themselves to be the core team "to spread the gospel and to plant a church." They asked Hollis to come and be their priest.

Kapolei is a mixed community, with many "locals" who can't afford a home elsewhere as well as others who include middle-income and support workers. While Hollis had the strengths of her energy and local connections in the community, she had never started a new congregation. She attended the "Plant My Church" training offered by the Episcopal Church in various locations around the country, and trained directly with Victoria Heard, a mission developer previously in the Diocese of Virginia and currently in the Diocese of Dallas.

But Hollis has found that, with the energy and devotion of the core congregation members, the mission has blossomed and flourished more quickly than many other church-plants. "It doesn't have to come from the priest—our folks don't expect me to be the point person for evangelism." When asked about evangelism at St. Nicholas', Hollis laughed and talked about how effortless it seemed among congregation members. "It's easier with new Christians. When you're moving from a black-and-white world to a Technicolor world, you say, 'Wow!' and you want to tell others." Their evangelism seemed to flow naturally out of their gratitude, not out of necessity or duty. "Our people tell their friends, neighbors, and colleagues things like, 'We've been going to church and our marriage is better.' That's evangelism." At St. Nicholas', evangelism has become an organic expression of the congregation's life—it is not programmatic, formulaic, or institutional. Their evangelism is motivated by joy, not by fear—and people do not confuse God's grace with church membership. "We don't say, 'You're going to hell if you don't go to church.'"

Bishop Fitzpatrick shares Hollis' perspective on the congregation: "They are not afraid anymore. They'll do door-to-door work, and deliver water bottles on the beach, and give donuts to people stuck in traffic. They've created a music ministry appropriate to the setting. They have a retired Filipino priest who helps with Filipino community—and it works because the grandchildren are *already* coming to the church, and with Father Tim Quintero there, the grandparents can come and connect more easily. They talk more about prayer and God than most congregations I work with. Individually, they express more about doing what they feel called to do, and they use phrases like 'my ministry.'"

At St. Nicholas' Church, Christian conversion and transformation are not one-time events. Members share a habit of dedication to living a Christian life, as pilgrims on a journey. "If you're living a Christian life, your life will change." Hollis and the original twelve have fostered a strong emphasis on small groups and covenant groups. Members see the covenant groups as the place where the gospel and their individual lives connect, where they have permission, time, and commitment to look at that connection more closely with each other. St. Nicholas' uses a model of covenant groups developed by Kevin Phillips in Mountain View, California.

"Evangelism on the edge means you look at every-thing," and for Hollis and the members of St. Nicholas' that includes worship, location, message, and time. Lay members and clergy have committed themselves to "evan-gelism on the edge," which for them means being real for the culture of their people, and being in that culture fully. "You have to *really* attend to the person you're trying to reach." For this community, in worship that means using new music with a lot of rhythm, played by a band and sung by vocalists, with words projected on a screen. While this is not Hollis' personal preference, she recognizes the importance of having the gospel spoken and sung in a language that can be heard and embraced by the people of the surrounding culture. "It doesn't matter what my tastes are. I have to leave my personal piety out of the church."

Worship is only one example of an overall approach to Christian living. At St. Nicholas', the focus is on truly knowing people and connecting with them where they are. "We know our people—what their life concerns are, where they work, what their kids are doing—and we connect to that." That has meant a change in Hollis's preaching, so that now she seeks to use examples that help people see how they can apply the gospel directly to their day-to-day lives. By taking this approach in the pulpit, Hollis also models for congregation members how to identify and talk about moments of God's grace in their lives—thus equipping them with some of the basic skills for an easy and natural spiritual practice of sharing good news.

HOLY SPIRIT, MARS HILL, NORTH CAROLINA
In the mountains of western North Carolina, in a small town with a Baptist college, a woman named Susan Sherard felt prompted to start a house church. Church of the Holy Spirit marks its beginning on September 8, 1985, with its first gathering of interested people in the Roman Catholic storefront in Mars Hill. It grew steadily over ten years to over 250 members, with 120 attending each week. By 2000, Holy Spirit was known throughout the county for its social outreach and community spirit.

Susan's desire to start a church in Madison County was quickly affirmed by people from various backgrounds with whom she discussed the idea. "I knew a lot of people who were not going to church because their spiritual lives were not compatible with the fundamentalist and hierarchical nature of churches in our area. Also, there were a lot of people in our county with basic needs and dreams of justice that were not being addressed. I thought an Episcopal ministry could touch both of those needs. So [the idea] slowly grew in me.... Really, my beginning of priesthood was the beginning of a notion to start a church, not so much a notion to be a priest. Then as I began to imagine it, I said something to just a few people, friends of mine, and they were all very taken by the idea. None of them were Episcopalians—they were in the community. Some of them are here today. Some joined, and some didn't.... And I saw that there were quite a few people not going to church who were intrigued by what Episcopal Church could offer."

> I don't think there's more than a handful at most of cradle Episcopalians in this church.... I guess I'd describe them as the people who question, who are not satisfied with the cut-and-dry church, or the traditional.
> — Elly, member of Church of the Holy Spirit, Mars Hill

Susan's original vision was not grand. She simply wanted to meet for intensive fellowship and discipleship, breaking bread, and prayer, with a small group of people. "I had imagined it would always be a house church, and that we would probably meet in my living room," where there would be mutual exploration of scripture and a focus on service to neighbors.

Susan continued to be surprised by "the numbers of people who were hungry for a faith community that allowed them to be who they were. That was at first rather shocking to me, because it automatically meant from the beginning that I was in for something much bigger than I thought." Even before their first meeting in the Catholic storefront, she knew that the first gathering would be larger than her living room could accommodate. "Every time we met, we would have worship, and we'd have supper, then we'd have a meeting where we talked.... Even people who would declare that they were not religious, and who would say they couldn't stand the institutional church—and I believed them!—they kept coming. And every time we met, there would be more and more. People were showing up and committing, who a year before would have sworn that they would have never done it—and I would have agreed that they would have never done it!"

Susan views the unfolding of Church of the Holy Spirit as a mutual pilgrimage. "I think the reason it has been so successful is that there was no 'Father or Mother knows best' in terms of how you do things. My spiritual leadership has always been respected from the beginning. But we were learning so much together, and I didn't have any reason to act as if I wasn't learning, too, because I so obviously was." Ideas and decisions were tested out in a group, and Susan firmly implanted a dialogical listening process for dealing with any conflict. Mutuality in decision-making and a sense of mutual pilgrimage gripped people's imaginations, and they adopted for themselves the scriptural image of God's people wandering in the wilderness.

There are many people who come because something is broken, and they feel this is a supporting community where there's a lot of love, and people will reach out and help you one to one—which, to me, in the long run, is more important than institutional ministries. People come because, pretty quickly, someone's going to end up reaching out to them, and there'll be caring going back and forth. — *Jerry, former senior warden, Church of the Holy Spirit, Mars Hill*

Susan also helped foster in people a natural practice of evangelism—naming the Holy in each other and in those they met. Susan said that this perspective was absolutely central to her faith and her entire approach to ministry. "It's a sustaining kind of picture: a belief in the engagement of God in people's lives that's very genuine—and proven daily to me—and that is not related to outcomes like who dies and who doesn't or who gets better and who doesn't and who is depressed and who isn't.... It's related to *evidence of engagement in the Holy.* I just see signs of it all around. That's the food—the promise that the Holy lives on earth and that we will encounter it."

Susan had no need to invent or make up these encounters with God in the lives of others around her. "It's so obvious all the time." But this perspective was also for Susan a deep habit, a personal discipline of faith. "I try, always, when I'm with someone, to find something in what they have said to me that at least tells me that they have *encountered* God. They don't have to *believe* it, but I will find some way to point that out, and they can take it or leave it." The practice began to take hold in the community through her example. "In meetings, I'll say it. And other people do it, too; it's not just me. It's allowed."

> At one point, we had 25 percent of our budget going to outreach. We helped start or fuel several human service projects in the county, and have a reputation for helping organize things. Our folks helped start the hospice agency. And we've been stalwarts in Habitat for Humanity and Neighbors in Need." — *Jerry, former senior warden, Church of the Holy Spirit, Mars Hill*

Susan's theology of grace might be described as *infectious.* Calling people to be open to the grace available to them each and every day, she reminds people that "grace is for us, but it's also for the purpose of God residing in us and then extending to others." For Susan, each person's encounter with the Holy is not just for that person, but will naturally lead to other people that person encounters experiencing God's presence. Furthermore, Susan and the members of Holy Spirit have found that this understanding of human relationship with God is truly unique in their setting—and it has led to some new challenges.

"In terms of loving God and neighbor as self," Susan claims, "there couldn't be a finer group of people. Some struggle with the creed, others with the language of scripture and the liturgy, some with certain aspects of the institution of the church. But these struggles are part of the journey, and, in a way, the questioning enlivens people's desire to be on the journey together. Sometimes I wonder

So TRUE!!!

if part of our calling is to remain rooted in the tradition while at the same time opening ourselves to the church that is yet to be created."

Susan has moved on in her ministry now, but this intensely questioning community, pledging themselves to continue on their pilgrimage together, has had a significant impact in the community—not in an institutional way, but as individuals and small groups known as "people from Holy Spirit." As Tom, the previous mayor, said, "The church communicates its message and mission less through the media and more through one-on-one connections with members who are active and involved in the life of the community at different levels—industry and entrepreneurship, volunteerism, social activism." People are known for their manner of living the Christian life, practiced in community.

---

the word in a new tongue: evangelizing new generations

Lay and ordained disciples are creating remarkable evangelistic ministries with young people in all sorts of communities and contexts. These stretch the identity of the Episcopal Church beyond its institutional habits—and we are all enriched. But because lay and ordained evangelists have dared to learn new ways of sharing good news, their ministries have not been automatically embraced by the institutional church. These four evangelistic efforts have thrived despite opposition or lack of interest, helping young people discover and share God's love.

THEOLOGY ON TAP
A program originally developed in a single Roman Catholic parish north of Chicago in 1980, Theology on Tap now is used nationally and internationally by

Catholics and Protestants. Organized locally by young adults for young adults, Theology on Tap continues to grow because of its emphasis on personal invitation, hospitality, the sharing of personal stories, and personal follow-up. Every year, over six thousand young adults participate in the Roman Catholic Archdiocese of Chicago alone—unique in American Roman Catholicism, where nationally there is a flight of young people from church involvement. In recent years, Episcopalians and Roman Catholics have teamed up to offer Theology on Tap at bars, coffeehouses, and parishes in the Chicago and San Francisco metropolitan areas.

> I went by myself; I didn't know exactly what to expect. So, I just decided to try it out—sat in the back, you know, easy access out if I didn't like it. . . . I had expected maybe twenty people in a classroom—and people I probably wouldn't associate with normally. And it wasn't like that at all. It was two hundred people my age, on a beautiful night, sitting in front of a Catholic Church, talking about things that were pretty relevant. That got me hooked on coming. The next time, I invited some friends. And we all went for the next three sessions. — *Derrick Jackson, age 27*

Theology on Tap started as a program at a Roman Catholic parish in a northwest suburb of Chicago. Younger members of the congregation, along with a younger priest, noticed the diminishing presence of young adults (ages eighteen to thirty-five) in congregational life and worship, and decided to do something about it. Instead of trying to get young adults to commit to existing parish programs and ministries—which were designed mostly for retired individuals and the families of middle-aged couples—they decided to create short-term gatherings based on the interests and yearnings of young adults themselves. They relied on their own God-given creativity, drawing from their stories and the stories of their peers to guide them in creating a series of young adult gatherings. They focused on bridging the gap between "sacred" and "secular," helping their peers—and themselves—recognize and name God's work in their daily lives.

Theology on Tap emerged during a time of evangelistic energy in the Catholic Archdiocese of Chicago, and has become its flagship program among its various ministries with young adults. "But we don't like to call it a program," says John Cusick, director of Young Adult Ministry in the Archdiocese of Chicago, who has dedicated his ministry to young adults since 1977. "We call Theology on Tap a 'speaker and discussion series.'" Even this simple nuance in language signals an underlying philosophy guiding Theology on Tap. It is a series with open drop-in atten-dance, not a program that requires people to sign up. It is structured, but dynamic; organized, but organic.

Now, every summer, over sixty-five parishes in the Chicago metropolitan area host Theology on Tap, with twenty to four hundred people attending speaker and discussion events at each site. Finding fresh engagement with Christian faith, many young adults have also returned to nearby parishes. Theology on Tap has had an impact on a number of parishes around the city, with churches like Old St. Pat's and St. Clement's, and in neighborhoods with a high density of young adults hosting standing-room-only Masses each Sunday. John Cusick made the philosophy of Theology on Tap very clear:

> The magic of Theology on Tap is that it becomes an event—an experience—and that in itself is worth the price of admission. You think you are coming to a program and you get caught up in something much larger than that. You're made to feel welcome. You are literally fed, you're given a beverage. You are allowed some dialogue. You're not told hurry up and get out of here. You're welcomed back. You might get a note in the mail thanking you for coming and inviting you back the next week. If Theology on Tap

works right, its magic is that it's a whole method-
ology to begin connecting younger people with the
greatness of the Christian story.

> If people come in on Sunday and all they hear is
> family-oriented things...they say, "I'm not family."
> And after over twenty years working in young
> adult ministry, I still find that young adults are
> not a priority in our churches. — *John Cusick*

Theology on Tap is offered for four consecutive weeks,
with speaker events each night of the week at different
churches throughout the metropolitan area. At each parish,
on a designated night each week, an invited speaker talks
about a topic connecting the life of faith with the significant life concerns of young adults—work, vocation, and
work ethics; relationships, sex, and family; money and
financial responsibility; life purpose and social impact; and
major global and national concerns. Speakers include well-
known clergy, laity, monastics, and scholars, of all ages. A
nun will give a talk on volunteerism and faith; a cartoonist
will speak about cultivating a conscience; a scholar will
lecture on Islam. The speaker then poses questions for
exploration, and asks the gathered group of young adults
to break into small discussion groups. After a break, the
speaker offers some summarizing thoughts and further
challenges, followed either by a second small group discussion or a full-group "Q & A" conversation.

Theology on Tap is explicitly for young adults. John
Cusick's hard-line position is that most church programs
and congregations are comprised of—and designed to
satisfy—"school-aged families and senior citizens."
Consequently, "there are more and more people today
who are not raising school-aged kids and who are not
senior citizens, and feel that they're not being ministered
to by their local church.... I'm the spokesperson for this
age group and therefore I have to constantly look at life

through the lens of somebody who's thirty-something or twenty-something. And so if I don't constantly listen to them, if I don't spend time with them and hear their needs, then I'm never going to look through their lens. That's the problem at most churches."

Young adults who attend Theology on Tap, at least at the more strongly committed parishes, find an experience unlike anything they have experienced in the Roman Catholic Church. The first impression is visual: "Here are people like me." The second impression is relational: with a high premium placed on the hosting parish's hospitality, young adults are greeted with a warm welcome, introduced to others, and given food and drink. The third impression is personal and spiritual: "Here are people like me, talking about things that I am struggling with, who are unashamed to talk about their faith."

Perry, age twenty-seven, described his first experience at Theology on Tap in this way:

> I had just gotten here from Mexico. I was doing a service project and I started school; I had never lived downtown, and so it was all new to me. I went to a bunch of churches just trying to find a fit, and I didn't. So when I came here that night, maybe it was because it was so personal. We were in a big group downstairs and you heard people talking and sharing. And right away I knew that I'd be coming to this church. The magic of Theology on Tap is that people get to know one another here.... For me it's just other people living a Christian life and that's something I've looked for and it's here. It's on display and you can find it. I mean, it just bridges well—the secular life and the Christian life. So many people have amazing jobs and amazing careers—but they're still here.

Central to Theology on Tap is the opportunity for young adults to connect with peers who have the courage and desire to explore important issues and share their stories with each other. Kate DeVries, program coordinator for the Archdiocesan Young Adult Ministries, said about Theology on Tap, "When you walk into the room, you can feel the excitement—or you can feel peace—or you can feel the tension, if it's an issue that people are struggling with. There's nothing flat about it. It evokes spirit. It evokes dynamism. The Spirit is very present."

This experience, connecting with peers and connecting day-to-day life with the Christian story, comes free of expectations. As John Cusick noted, "The church is not asking them to do anything but show up." But the total experience of welcome, hearing good news spoken in the language and events of everyday life, and seeing others take the risky step of sharing personal life with peers entices young adults, awakening their awareness of the Holy Spirit at work.

Theology on Tap depends on personal contact. Young adult planners learn the basics of evangelism and become comfortable talking about Christian faith with their peers, including those who had left or never experienced Christianity. Every planning team member is charged with inviting at least four people in person. A side benefit of this approach is that the group that gathers for Theology on Tap already has some degree of connectedness, easing the anxiety about sharing stories of pilgrimage with each other in small groups. Perry's experience speaks to the value of sharing life stories with his peers:

> Breaking down to small groups is just such a great idea. I mean, when you're doing it, you're like, "Oh my God, no way do I want to do this!" But when you do it, it adds a whole new element to the night. What was a passive-listening evening becomes a very active sharing evening.

The experience of leading, planning, and speaking at Theology on Tap is transformative. Young adult planners learn basic skills and develop courage for sharing their faith; young speakers learn what they have to offer from their own pilgrimages. Danielle, an articulate teacher and community organizer in Chicago, said:

> When Father Cusick asked me to speak at Theology on Tap, I said, "What do I have to offer a group of people? What am I going to say to these people?" He said, "You've just got to say what is important to you." He said he could get up and speak for forty-five minutes about spirituality, just like that. But he's a priest, and that's what people expect him to say. But he really wanted the talks to come from everyday people. And so when I was up there speaking, though I was nervous, I told people, "This is what I do on a day-to-day basis" and "This is how I live my life." I said, "This is my story."

More seasoned speakers are also transformed by Theology on Tap, because it challenges them to make real, clear connections between faith and everyday life. John talked about his own ongoing transformation: "They've taught me to reexamine everything about my own Catholic faith. You cannot sell something that you do not understand yourself. How young adult people have challenged me is, 'Do you believe that?' and, 'How does it work in your life?'"

And finally, young adults' ideas about religious gathering are transformed. At St. Clement's Church, where Theology on Tap is held outside on the front lawn, young adults experience not only the joy of sharing their stories with each other and talking about important issues in the cool of summer evenings, but they also experience the gaze of passersby who notice them gathered together. Through this experience, they begin to develop an image of the church not as institution, but as a community of people who live their lives of faith publicly, who simply by gathering create a public witness to Christ.

While serving a congregation north of Chicago, I had the pleasure of working with an energetic team of young adults who first introduced Theology on Tap at an Episcopal parish. We committed ourselves enthusiastically to the planning process, including learning basic skills of evangelism. We also got our own rotation of speakers, who could speak to the Christian experience from a more broadly ecumenical as well as Anglican perspective. With a team of six, we hosted four great weeks of Theology on Tap. In our first year, we had fifty to sixty people every week. Energy was high, and one of the young moms on the team said to me, "This is the most fun I've had at this church, ever!"

We found out quickly that people responded to a good and exciting series by returning to our church on Sunday to check it out. Several came once and left, disappointed that they did not find a similar level of engagement and welcome on Sunday morning. But several others stayed, connected with people at our parish, and found a spiritual home.

In each of the three following years our attendance dropped a bit. We had lost the primary focus on the risk of personal invitation. We had begun to treat Theology on Tap as a program and had slipped toward making it for *us* rather than for our peers. And we encountered rising resistance and resentment from some influential long-term parish members who did not appreciate something being offered that did not include them. No program, however good it is, solves the evangelism challenge. What is needed is an enduring change of heart, where proclaiming good news becomes a joyful spiritual habit among young and old alike.

A linked youth group has blossomed in the past seven years in the two small northeastern Arizona communities of Winslow and Holbrook. The group, comprised of Navajo and white youth, has grown to nearly 50 percent of the average Sunday attendance of the two parishes combined. This growth is the result of young people's commitment to finding God in their everyday lives, their invitation to peers based on their own experiences of God's love, and their deep trust in the work of Kaze Gadaway, a newcomer whom they call "Grandmother." "We just had three baptisms of young people who have been in the youth group for one year," Kaze reported. "And this was their idea. That's three this year—and ten baptisms of young people in the last five years."

Kaze found herself drawn into ministry with youth in these two neighboring communities shortly after she moved to Arizona. She had attended a diocesan conference aiming to strengthen parish youth ministries. "I remember them asking, almost apologetically and kind of embarrassed, if anyone would be willing to lead youth work in Holbrook and Winslow. I volunteered—and they were kind of shocked that anyone would volunteer." Previous to Kaze's arrival, there had been a very small youth group at each of these small parishes, St. Paul's in Winslow and St. George's in Holbrook. These youth groups had died not only because of loss of interest but, more significantly, from deep wounding of young people through sexual and physical abuse.

Kaze first talked to people in each congregation and compiled a contact list of all young people currently or previously associated with the congregations. She then contacted these young people's parents, asking if their children would be interested in a new youth group. Most parents said no, but Kaze persisted, asking to talk to their children directly, and setting up appointments to meet young people face to face in their homes. They responded positively and the youth group started with about ten and fifteen people, at their first combined retreat. Today, there are two youth groups again, with about fifteen attending each youth group regularly, and ten more young people "in the background" of each.

Church members were initially uneasy about this infusion of young people into their communities. "A lot of people are scared of youth," Kaze told me. "Adults in the congregations said to me, 'What if they ask me about faith or something like that? I wouldn't know what to say.' I was shocked. They also told me that they didn't know how to talk to youth informally, like at potlucks." Kate could not understand people's difficulty, having spent her career as a teacher and community developer, working with gangs and other young people in underprivileged communities in Chicago and in other countries.

"I know how to talk with young people, and what they expect. They are *honest* about what they're thinking—and people get scared of that kind of honesty. They have *real questions*—they are *not* into circular thinking or abstractions (you know, like 'We know God loves us because God is love and love is the basis of everything,' that kind of thinking). They want to know, 'If God loves me and I ask to stop being beaten, why didn't God stop it from happening?' They aren't interested in the Trinity, or the Good Shepherd. They want to know if God will look for them when they are lost—really. They are interested in the bottom line. Last year a friend of theirs died in a car accident, and they began asking, 'If we had prayed for him to be safe beforehand, would God have saved him from dying?' So, I look to them to help find answers. I ask questions—and then they come alive and respond."

Kaze began the youth ministry with a focus on prayer—prayer as intense and real conversation with God, grounded in the events of every day. The youth latched on to this way of thinking about prayer, and they bring the events of their lives into discussion and mutual prayer. The process of discussing and reflecting on prayer transforms them, helping them become attuned to the movement of the Holy Spirit in their day-to-day life.

Young people are invited to be brutally honest with God—to express their confusion, rage, or sense of betrayal as well as their trust. One exercise that opens up this level of honesty is the "card game" (an idea Kaze took from "Peer Ministry Resources" shown at an Episcopal youth event). Young people create a deck of cards with personal questions about prayer and spiritual life (for example, "Have you ever experienced an angel?"; "Have you ever hated God?"; "Has anyone ever prayed for you?"). Then they take turns drawing cards and responding to them, using them as ways to tell each other stories of their relationships with God. Another exercise that helps young people enter this kind of honesty and also open themselves to ongoing transformation is writing their own versions of the Psalms: "Tell about a situation and describe it, then write about how God came to you and helped you, then end with praise to God."

Kaze is willing to go to the "dirty" places of young lives—abundant in a community where poverty, alcoholism, and abuse are part of the fabric of daily life. She has responded to desperate calls by both youth and adults, going to people's homes even when police are arriving at the scene. Some girls in the youth group have had unwanted pregnancies. Some boys are under house arrest. "I do not condemn them. I'm not their judge. I come to them and say, 'Where do we go from here?' And they *know* I will do this, and that I won't judge them." Kaze is a fellow pilgrim. "I have shared my own story of alcoholism with them. I'm in my sixteenth year of sobriety. The kids hear that and begin to talk about how maybe that's possible for them, too. They know I believe that they can start over any time, and that God is a God of new beginnings."

The young people—Native American, Latino, and white—have given her the name "Grandmother." "I think it's because of my consistency. I've stayed with them for six years, and plan to continue. I don't condemn them for what they do—and they do some pretty wild and wooly stuff. They know I pray for them."

> To me, evangelism is, they can see God in many situations, and they know how to talk about it to themselves and to others. — *Kaze Gadaway*

The heart of Kaze's ministry with youth is inviting them into the practice of naming the Holy. "My view of evangelism with kids is opening their eyes to how God is moving in their lives and how they respond back to God in prayer." Kaze's aim is to be a catalyst for God's transformation of how they look at life by introducing them to a deep practice of prayer that is concrete, visceral, and grounded in the reality of their lives. She wants young people to develop a different way of seeing things, in partnership with God. "I base this on something a rabbi said," Kaze explained. "'When we pray, we increase our capacity to see God at work and know more what to ask.' Our young people now understand this and are looking for it—in homeless people, in themselves, in the events of their lives and their families—and they are talking back to God. They are moving from a 'give me' mentality in prayer to a 'God appears' perspective. And that's wonderful to see—because I'm trying to invite them to look for the profound, the miraculous, the shaking and revealing in their lives."

◆　◆　◆　◆　◆

Alongside this youth ministry led by Kaze Gadaway, a center of care, shelter, and good news for homeless people arose in the Winslow and Holbrook area about fifteen years ago. It was the fruit of the heartfelt prayers of another woman who, new to Holbrook in her life pilgrimage, was prompted by God to bring together religious communities and create Holbrook's ecumenical Bread of Life Mission.

> A neighbor joked with me, "Mary, you can't be an evangelist! You're an Episcopalian!" But it's what I'm called to be. During the ministry of one of our prior priests, who really emphasized the ministry of all the baptized, I found a sense of what needed to be done. There were people freezing to death each year in Holbrook. I found a real heart for these people—the homeless and poor of Holbrook.

Mary Wilderman moved to Holbrook over twenty years ago from Peoria, Illinois, and quickly noticed the severe poverty and lack of resources there and in the neighboring communities. She found herself moved from compassion to action when she heard about—and witnessed—homeless and very poor people who froze to death.

Mary began praying with people in the Holbrook congregation about her awakening passion for ministry and her concern for people. After one year in prayer, she and others launched Bread of Life Mission. They started creating winter shelters, first at abandoned gas stations, then at area firehouses. Now, they have a thirty-bed emergency housing facility that operates year-round on forty acres purchased with funds provided by the state, and an ecumenical chapel. It is the only homeless shelter in the county, and serves not only many long-term homeless people in the county but also many transient homeless and mentally ill who come from Interstate 40 to Holbrook.

They have chapel services every night, led by different clergy and laity from many partnering denominations.

After years of service to Bread of Life, Mary has partly retired. She is still the board president, but now goes there only twice a week to work and do a chapel service. "We lost some more fundamentalist churches and groups," Mary noted. "They seemed to believe that once people heard the gospel and accepted Christ, they'd automatically stop drinking and get their lives together. When that didn't happen...well, they decided to focus their energy elsewhere. I preach grace, and they like that. So, many of them come to the Episcopal Church. And the Episcopal Church has been very receptive to the homeless. Some have become longer-term members. One is a member of the Bishop's Committee."

> We don't focus on denominational differences. We just lift up Jesus. Our homeless folks get a chance to experience and hear different approaches to Christian faith.
> — Mary Wilderman

The youth groups from both congregations have volunteered at Bread of Life Mission several times, including Mary's Native American godchildren. The Winslow and Holbrook congregations are small, and they have each lost some beloved long-term members in recent years, due to denominational strife. Mary says, "The church has become very small since we moved here—about fifteen families total. After the 2003 General Convention, seven families left, cutting our church almost in half." Mary laments the loss of these friends, and hopes they may return. But she—and Kaze—also remain unflagging in their evangelistic and life-giving ministries.

"THE OFFICE"
This vibrant African-American Episcopal campus ministry at the State University of New York (SUNY) at

Buffalo, once among the largest mainline Christian campus ministries in the country, grew and thrived through personal invitation to its witness as a vibrant and organic community of faith, with at least fifty students involved each school year. In 2002, its diocese discontinued the ministry's funding. A nearby parish learned, too late, of its imminent demise, and attempted to rescue and rebuild the ministry. But the wounds had already cut deeply, and the gathered community of African-American students dispersed. At its restart after closure, the Episcopal campus ministry had one white student involved. The following is a tribute to this evangelistic ministry in its full vibrancy—and a cautionary tale for our dioceses.

In 1994, Beverly Moore-Tasy, a recently ordained priest, arrived on the SUNY-Buffalo campus to build and strengthen an Episcopal campus ministry. As the only African-American chaplain on campus, she developed an immediate affinity with African-American students, and together with her assistant, Linda Wilson, helped create a community of care, friendship, fun, and discipleship that became infectious among students. Her full-time chaplaincy was contingent on a three-year grant, and by the end of the three years, independent funding had not been secured, and Beverly needed to resign. For the next five years, the Episcopal Campus Ministry at SUNY-Buffalo continued on a shoestring budget through the dedicated service of Linda Wilson, the students who found life in this community, and an interim half-time chaplain, Lorna Williams. The ministry touched the lives of students across the campus, including the twenty to thirty students who came to its offices each day. By 1999, over fifty students were regularly involved in ministry activities. As a previous board member stated, "I think it's recognized on the campus as being not only the most successful, but probably the *only* accessible support ministry with a

Christian base that's available on campus for minority students."

When I first visited "The Office"—the name given to the Episcopal Campus Ministry, for its location in three rooms of a small shopping center on campus—I met a dynamic group of young people eager to gather with one another, talk about their lives, sing, study, and read the Bible. Rarely have I encountered people with such freedom and ease in expressing their faith, sharing their stories, and celebrating God's good news. The students themselves were the primary evangelists. After just a little while in The Office, where newcomers were immediately welcomed and invited to join in the community's freeform conversations that flowed naturally in and out of discussions of Christian faith and discipleship, students found themselves eager to tell their friends about The Office and invite them to come.

It is little wonder that students were enthusiastic about the community: at The Office, they experienced freedom, good humor, and enjoyment of each other; they found a space they could call their own and the permission to create their own shared ministry with each other; they found their full humanity welcomed with delight, honor, and a willingness to wrestle together with difficulties. Linda Wilson described the tone well when she said, "I think that on a college campus of over thirty thousand people, it's hard to find a place where there's so much laughter."

Linda was a lynchpin for this vibrant fellowship of sojourners. Linda, who was not originally an Episcopalian but who fell in love with the ministry for which she worked, became the students' *de facto* chaplain. She served as a steady "constant," a person students could always count on to be there. She got to know each student personally. "What I want students to come away with from here is that they can come back, that there is a place here on campus where we're not going to turn our backs on you.

There's a place here on campus where if you really need food, we're going to help you find it. If you're lonely, well, we'll try and find you a friend." Linda became involved in students' lives and related to them as fellow pilgrims— people with dignity. Jessi, a graduating senior, talked about how Linda related to the student community:

> Sometimes she brings her kids and it's just a family atmosphere. She cooks for us. She talks to us. She reasons with us. Sometimes you would look at her and be like, "Well, how does she identify with all these kids from so many different backgrounds?" But she relates to anyone. . . . She has that connection with us without being artificial or forced. She meets us where we are.

Linda's straightforward manner appealed to students. They sought her out for advice and care, and described her at times like a mother. But they also interacted with her as a trusted friend, telling her things they did not feel free to tell their own families. Linda was not always gentle; when necessary she told students what they needed to hear. Sylvia Correra, an engineering student, described her experience of The Office as her salvation, and Linda played no small part in this:

I don't think I would have made it in engineering if it wasn't for this Office, There's many times that I felt like saying, "You know what, Linda, I give up. I just don't want to do it anymore." She was like, "You know what, you get back in there, you pick yourself up and you do your work." And I was like, "But you don't understand." She was like, "No, I understand perfectly—you go up there, you can do it, don't let a GED hold you back."

Sylvia's testimony goes far beyond her experiences with Linda. Sylvia's history as a high school dropout from the projects in New York City left her feeling like she didn't really have a family. For her, the community of The

Office—a community of people who were each on a life pilgrimage—gave her a whole range of experiences she had never had before. Sylvia was spiritually awakened. "To be honest with you," she said, "I don't think I've felt love like this before. What happens if I don't come in at a certain time, when I usually come in? 'Oh, where's Sylvia? She hasn't come in today.' This group loves me. I know they love me, I feel it, and I love them too. That's the most important thing, I think, is the love that we share and we have for one another."

> This place actually got me saved, you know. I learned how to live like a Christian, act like a Christian. I was so mean when I was back at home, I was just so vindictive, and I had the wrong attitude. I came to UB— you know, what would have happened if I hadn't come to the Episcopal Campus Ministry? Would I still be the same person, would I still be just as vindictive?
> — Sylvia Correra, student, age 28, student

Many of the students involved in The Office did not grow up as Christians, much less as Episcopalians. Some had grown up in Christian homes and churches but had never developed any interest in the church. Others had never experienced Christian community or heard the stories. Dex Hutchinson, who found his way to The Office after struggling with a football injury, talked about how his mother and grandmother were faithful Christians who presented him with the Christian faith from a young age.

My grandmother was very religious—always gave us Bibles for Christmas. We didn't want to have anything to do with that, because she was forceful with it.... My mother's [evangelism] was mostly just playing her music, basically being an example, reading her Bible. Me and my mother had a really close relationship and at times I would go in her room to just hang out, and she was like, "Dex, this is my personal time." I never understood that until

I came to school and when I gave my life to Christ. So...as a result of my mother just being an example and just allowing me, I came on my own.

Dex did not expect to find God during college. "I definitely wasn't looking for God. Actually, I had been one who had totally given up on God. Not just God, Christ, but God, period. God, that there was a creator. So that wasn't on my mind. I wasn't really here for education, wasn't here for friends. I wanted to be an engineer, but I didn't have much motivation to be one. I would say I was walking blindly and here is where I found Christ, so he was obviously leading me."

Students were brought by friends to The Office, or heard about it through the grapevine and just showed up. Many were transformed by the welcome, the sharing of stories, the respect, and the playful and joyful expressions of Christian faith. Some became leaders in the community, seeking in their own ways to enrich the spiritual life of their fellow sojourners. One returning student started a men's ministry group on campus and also helped create a space in The Office for prayer. "I basically came up with the concept of the prayer room because a lot of times students would come back here and just use this as their quiet time, a place for them to worship and just get down on their knees and pray. So I took it to Linda, and we established this. And we have a book of prayers back here—and even if students don't pray they write their name or whatever they need to be prayed for in that book. And those who do pray on a routine basis, they'll come back and check it often."

Energy spread among the students. Sylvia, experiencing her own transformation, wanted to "give back what was given to me at the beginning. There's always new members coming in here, and we have to set an example for them—because we were in the same shoes they were in. We're always here, open all day, and if you ever feel stressed, you can always feel free to come in here. Any stranger can come in here and just say, 'Can someone pray with me?' and someone's always here to pray with them." Another student said, "We really do stand out. When we had the September 11th tragedy, we were the first ministry on campus that actually had a prayer vigil, and this whole room was filled."

Sylvia expressed the tremendous hope and anxiety of any pilgrim who has encountered Christ and been awakened to God's grace. On the one hand, she wanted to continue to give back as she had received—"I'm doing excellent and I feel the reason why I'm doing so good is because of God and because of my motivation. . . . And I want to give back to ECM, if it's still here." On the other hand, Sylvia was afraid of losing what she had gained—"I'm really afraid of getting derailed. I'm really afraid of going back to what I used to be and I don't want to go back there anymore. I know that life. I ran the streets for a couple of years and I know that it's not for me. [And] here, I was looking for a family, you know—and I got a family. So what am I going to do now when I leave, where am I going to find a family?"

Due to a loss of institutional church support, The Office closed its doors in 2002. I was not able to find out what has become of the students involved.

FAITH INKUBATORS

A Lutheran pastor, frustrated with traditional and over-institutionalized Sunday school approaches to Christian formation, helped start Faith Inkubators, an ecumenical ministry based in Minnesota focused on training parents to raise their children with daily practices of Christian faith. Today, over one thousand congregations—Lutheran as well as from many other denominations—participate in the Faith Inkubators process of helping families learn how to nurture faith "every night in every home," as a practice of continuing evangelism.

When Rich Melheim was a teenager, he had a profound conversion experience that led him to deeper faith and shaped his entire focus as a disciple and minister. As a pastor, he began working with teenagers: "American teens are the biggest mission field in the world!" In his first position, he took over for a youth minister who had been dismissed for sexual impropriety.

During his time as a youth pastor, two teenage boys in his youth group committed suicide and Rich's entire focus of ministry changed. As he grieved their deaths and wrestled with the question of what might have saved them, he realized that a program approach to youth ministry and a focus on single weekly encounters with teens was not enough. He started to build a systemic network that would surround teenagers and children with "multiple redundant faith ministers"—people through whom teens and kids would encounter Christian faith and witness every day in multiple places. The concept that formed the core of Faith Inkubators' purpose was born—helping parents create habits of faith and prayer with their children, "every night in every home." "We moved out of the classroom and into a faith journey mentality"—a shift from an institutional approach to a focus on journeying with teenagers and children as fellow pilgrims.

In 1993, Rich wrote an article titled, "Conformation (sic!) is Dead." It was like Martin Luther nailing his Ninety-five Theses to the Wittenberg Church door. Within months, responses poured in, with over a hundred speaking invitations. Within a year, 270 churches had recreated their entire process of faith formation for children and teenagers. Rich left parish ministry to lead this new movement, and by the end of two years, 540 congregations had adopted the approach he and others designed. By 2007, Faith Inkubators had been embraced by thousands of Lutheran congregations with teens and adapted for use in thirteen different denominations.

One of the core approaches designed by Faith Inkubators is "Faith Stepping Stones," an aid that helps parents build worship and prayer as a pattern of life with their children. Rich and others worked to create a process for introducing developmentally meaningful rituals of worship and prayer with children. Parents learn in three-week classes at their churches about emotional, physical, and spiritual development of their children at different stages. They also learn rituals of prayer, worship, and reflection to introduce at each stage, such as blessing the child each night, praying thanksgivings and sharing stories about each day, learning to reflect spiritually on life, to repent and forgive others. This process helps children develop natural habits of faithful conversation with God and each other.

Faith Inkubators' concept of church is distinctly noninstitutional. As Rich said, "Your heart is a church, and your home is a church, and your extended adopted family is a church, and each small group in the congregation is a church. You have experienced God in multiple places before you ever get to the fifth level of church—the whole congregation." To foster this multilayered experience of church, Faith Inkubators encourages each household to build what Rich calls "a true house-church—where every home is a church." Each household forms a faith family of twelve people ("Generations in Faith Together"), with at least one person in each living generation—not necessarily blood relatives—gathering together regularly for meals, prayer, reflection, and worship. Families are invited to commit to constantly recreating, extending, and adopting family members who share their table with them—and older members of congregations are invited to offer themselves as surrogate grandparents. This larger faith family then helps reinforce what parents practice with their children in Faith Stepping Stones as well as bringing down to earth what is shared in the congregation. Likewise, the congregation reinforces—but does not replace—the work of families in nurturing faith.

Christian parents are charged with the honor and responsibility to raise their children to know Jesus. The church should help them, but not do the job for them. The family is a church… and must be inspired, challenged, and trained to model all the functions of the church (education, proclamation, prayer, acts of loving service, etc.) in the home. —*www.faithink.com*

Rich has gathered a staff, lay leaders, and clergy who are passionate about walking with children and helping them develop a language of faith. Rich is fond of quoting author and Franciscan friar Brennan Manning to express how Faith Inkubator leaders are committed to keeping this approach spiritually rooted and connected to their own experiences of God's love: "Unless all this is incarnate in me, I'm just a travel agent handing out brochures for places I've never been." Deb Streicher, a lay leader who serves her ELCA synod as the representative for evangelism, developed her evangelistic passion through her work with Faith Inkubators. "I personally have grown to be an evangelist because of a system that sets expectations for growing faith in the home and develops the understanding of fostering a nurturing community where that faith can grow. When you see how it can work, you're willing to serve more. And then you see children respond—and the end result is that you evangelize because you understand what this faith is all about."

Deb never expected to become so engaged in the spiritual practice of evangelism. But she found in Rich's work a deep connection with her own experience as a teacher. "I didn't go through all those years living in other countries just to learn how to speak and teach other languages. I was learning about how to share the faith." Deb described the Faith Stepping Stones approach in light of her experience teaching language.

> Before my work with the church, I taught Spanish and Japanese both in school and after school. And parents continually came to me and asked, "When will my child become fluent?" And I replied, "Well, can you let them live in a country where they will be immersed in the language?" So I went to the county administration and asked to do a parent-child language class. And the county said yes. These parents no longer asked when their kids would become fluent—instead, they found their own hurdles, excuses, and reasons for why they weren't getting their own work done and becoming fluent themselves. . . . In order to become fluent in a language, you need to be immersed, surrounded in the home, and speak and sing. And then, you become drawn to the language you've learned. It is the same with the language of faith. Why do we expect it to be any different?

Deb described how these various approaches aim to foster "theologically sound small groups that pray together, speak their stories to each other, and learn scripture." These shared stories become the central evangelistic experiences. Deb shared with me the story of Maia, a one-year-old girl growing up with parents who started practicing what was learned while attending the Faith Stepping Stones. "When it came time for the blessing, Maia crawled over and made the sign of the cross on her four-year-old brother's head. She continued to insist on doing this for her brother at every bedtime, and wanted her brother to do the same for her."

She admits that the Faith Inkubators approaches have not worked in some congregations but thinks it may be due more to the habits and assumptions of church members.

> It's because they haven't set expectations, or they treat the expectations as suggestions and only occasionally adopt them. They aren't adopting the actual practices and disciplines in everyday life. When we ask why children aren't responding, we hear things like "Well, we share highs and lows sometimes, but not always," or "See, we don't have a lot of Bibles here," or "I'm not the pastor—how am I supposed to apply scripture to my life?" This is no way to learn a language!

Faith Inkubators has been used in varying ways by Episcopal parishes in Pennsylvania, Virginia, Illinois, California, and other states, helping parents relearn (or learn anew) the spiritual practice of continuing evangelism—so they can fulfill the promises they made at their children's baptism. It is one of several approaches (the Youth and Family Institute, also in Minnesota, is another) developed by Lutherans and other denominations to empower parents for their God-graced work of raising their children in faith.

programmatic *and* personal?

Congregations around the country have adopted programs developed explicitly for faith renewal and for parish-based evangelism. Four of the most common programs—Alpha, Via Media, Faith Alive, and Cursillo—have helped church members renew their faith, think about the work of evangelism, and develop personal language for their own faith journey. If judged by how well these programs reach people with no church connection or faith background, none seem to be very evangelistic. Church members involved in these programs often struggle with the personal responsibility expected of them to invite others to program events. But, if viewed in light of how faithful Christians become more comfortable talking about their experiences of God and developing greater sensitivity to people who have no faith, then these programs are indeed successfully evangelistic.

Two very different congregations—St. John's in Naples, Florida, and St. Bartholomew's in New York City—use at least two of these programs as a way to help people claim and renew their own faith, and invite "unchurched" friends, colleagues, and neighbors into an encounter with Christian faith. St. John's uses Alpha and Cursillo. St. Bartholomew's uses Via Media and Cursillo, and has used an adapted Alpha program.

Alpha: An evangelistic teaching and discussion program from the Church of England, offering people a "primer" course in Christianity

Cursillo: A renewal and immersion retreat program from the Roman Catholic Church, bringing people together for intensive retreats and faith renewal

Via Media: An evangelistic teaching program from the Episcopal Church, raising basic questions about the connection of faith to our experience

These programs structure time and space for informal connections, the sharing of stories, and discussion of challenging questions, often around the context of a shared meal. They provide informative and at times provocative introductions to different aspects of the Christian faith. And, because of how topics are engaged and conversation unfolds, these programs bring people face to face with God's call in their lives, personally and individually.

Together with other experiences and ministry opportunities in a congregation, programs like these can generate renewed enthusiasm and clarity of commitment in members. It can still be challenging for members to find ways to adopt evangelism as a personal spiritual practice, and one must watch out for programs becoming substitutes for the real and challenging one-on-one engagement each of us might have with others in the world.

<hr />

evangelism becoming part of congregational identity

Even stalwart, well-established parishes can find themselves transformed into evangelistic communities where God's good news is shared and the Holy is welcomed and named. This has been the experience of four congregations we will consider here: St. Timothy's in Mountain View, California; St. Peter's in McKinney and St. Paul's in Waco, Texas; and All Saints' Church in Chicago, Illinois. Consistent to all of these—and many other churches across the country—are their emphases on seeking Christ in scripture, their own lives, their communities, and each other. The congregations range in size from two hundred to six hundred average Sunday attendance.

ST. TIMOTHY'S, MOUNTAIN VIEW, CALIFORNIA

> We are a growing, gospel-focused parish in the Silicon Valley; a covenant community united for worship, discipleship, and evangelism.

As this statement from its website affirms, St. Timothy's has transformed itself from a program-oriented but uncertain congregation to one that has embraced mission, evangelism, and outreach to people in the Silicon Valley as its central purpose. Their former rector, Kevin Phillips, helped spark this transformation, but since his departure St. Timothy's has continued to focus on covenant community and evangelism. In looking for a new leader, parishioners listed evangelism repeatedly as one of the key desired skills for a new rector in three core pastoral responsibilities: gospel-based visionary leadership, clear and applicable preaching, and lay leadership development.

How did this passion for evangelism develop? Kevin and others helped people make direct connections between the gospel and their daily lives, beginning with a focus on inner transformation and forming natural habits of sharing faith. Through preaching, Bible study and covenant groups for congregation members, and a ministry of theological reflection for business professionals, the people of St. Timothy's developed into a community capable of unique evangelistic witness to the high-powered professionals and scientists who live and work in Mountain View and the surrounding communities. Their approach to covenant groups and business-and-spirituality gatherings has been adopted in churches and communities across the country.

Kevin invited members of the congregation into a spiritual discipline of evangelism by first challenging them "to engage the faithfulness of God, that day by day they may be touched by transforming love so that they may touch others." Beginning with the covenant between God and Abram, he invited others to recognize and delight in God's blessings on their community and to share those blessings with the world around them. Through a course for lay leaders, *Making Disciples through Bible Study,* key members learned to listen for the movement of the Holy Spirit in their lives and explore their own sense of purpose in God's redemptive work. Those who were involved said, "The course was transformational"—and they became the messengers of this disciple-making process to the rest of the congregation.

Lay leaders and clergy teamed up to create two programs to help foster a spirit of evangelism: covenant groups and the Business Leadership Spirituality Network. Covenant groups, begun in 1994, connected people through discussion about their relationships with God and their lives of faith. Central to the covenant group experience was the sharing of stories and naming the Holy with one another. "We check in with one another sharing a high-point and a low-point of the week. We follow with a discussion centered on a subject arising out of real life. And we pray together."

Listening to God and Each Other (Mark 6:1–6)
+ *"Look"* (look at your own life): "Have you ever been frustrated by someone not really hearing you?"
+ *"Book"* (look at scripture): "How are Jesus' neighbors and family shortchanged by seeing who Jesus *was*, rather than who he *is*?"
+ *"Took"* (apply to life of faith): "How can we listen to God and each other with our souls fully engaged? How can we nurture sparks of faith in each other?"
— *Sample Questions from St. Timothy's Covenant Group*

Through experience in covenant groups, members developed natural habits of talking about their faith with one another. They also learned to do this with "strangers." Individuals regularly invited newcomers to these groups. And by attending, newcomers found themselves welcomed into profound, frank, and open conversations about the meaning in life.

Lay leaders were invited to use their talents and skills for evangelism and community enrichment. In response, they created retreat ministries, revitalized adult education, and a focus on spiritual growth. Through the teamwork of clergy, seminarians, and lay leaders, St. Timothy's formed the Business Leadership Spirituality Network (BLSN) in 2000, which now has Leadership Formation Groups of business professionals in Mountain View, California, and Boston, Massachusetts. Meeting together in groups of ten to twelve, business leaders reflect with one another on how to meet the challenges of ethical business practice and strengthen one another's leadership as Christians. The Leadership Formation Groups enter their discussion with one another through a process of *lectio divina*—meditation and reflection on a passage from scripture.

The goal of BLSN "is to infuse spirituality at the highest levels of business."[21] In their format, process, and aims they have drawn on the work of Andre Delbecq and John Huntington, business professionals who have committed themselves in university and church to foster spiritual maturity and faithful action among business leaders. Group discussions are held by members as confidential, so that a community of trust, support, and challenge can be fostered. A lay leader in the congregation, Mary Jo Alderson, has been involved with BLSN groups since the ministry began. BLSN has moved beyond a focus on business leaders alone. These leaders chose in 2007 to work in cooperation with the City of Mountain View to sponsor a "Transitions Seminar" at St. Timothy's to help people facing job-loss and other job-related problems by providing assistance with finances, family, and career reevaluation.

ALL SAINTS' CHURCH, CHICAGO, ILLINOIS

> There's a whole bunch of people in the world who are longing for God, this sense of God, this sense of being loved, and they want to make a difference. . . . My thought was to get the folks here thinking about something beyond themselves, and thinking about how they can use the gospel to change people's lives. (Bonnie Perry)

All Saints' Church was reborn in the 1990s. Before the new vicar arrived, it had fewer than thirty members. As a young priest with only a few years' experience, Bonnie Perry was uncertain about coming to work with All Saints'. But the remaining people had faced honestly the possibility that their parish might die, and they also held a deep hope for rebirth. While praying for wisdom and clarity, Bonnie realized that All Saints' was poised to offer incredible ministry in a quickly changing urban setting. While discerning whether or not to come to All Saints', she saw a paper sign posted on the front of the church with a picture of a phoenix rising from the ashes. The sign read: "All Saints': a Rising Church for the Risen Christ." Bonnie said, "I thought to myself, any church that can have a logo like that—well, there's something here."

The stories of congregational rebirth and growth at All Saints' are noteworthy: 35 percent of the congregation is in their twenties to mid-forties, and average attendance reached two hundred in 2004. This growth is an outward expression of inward change and a renewed focus on sharing God's good news. Bonnie saw an opportunity to gather the new, young energy in the neighborhood around a witness to God's mission centering in social concern and community-building. This meant becoming a very different kind of church community that did not "mirror" mainline church culture.

Bonnie began building a spirit of evangelism by listening. She visited everybody she could for one-on-one conversations like those community organizers have: "I went out to lunch with everybody. I just hung out with people. You find out what people's passions are and then you begin to find people who share those same passions, and you connect these people. It's amazing how far you can go when you don't try to impose your own great ideas on everyone." From these conversations, Bonnie learned what people in and beyond her congregation really cared about and how they sensed God speaking to them.

Bonnie then began prompting people to use their creativity to reach out to people in the surrounding neighborhood. The congregation advertised the church in Chicago's free classified advertisement press, *The Reader,* which was read widely by young adults and people new to the city. They began sponsoring an annual 5K run, offering refreshments at the end of the race and hosting worship. They started a new food ministry, providing free food to people in the community and offering a weekly free dinner that concluded with a shared Eucharist. When an insect blight resulted in the quarantine and destruction of historic trees in the neighborhood, All Saints' offered a memorial service for the trees. Parish members found varied ways to offer Christ's love, walk daily life with others around them, connect the sacred and secular, and be a community of fellow pilgrims with the people of their city. "That's what's valuable—if it actually offers some tangible means of living out the gospel, so they can see that as a result of their beliefs some things in the world have changed."

Bonnie's passion for evangelism comes from her own experience of deep gratitude, her awakening to God's amazing love. As a teenager, Bonnie went to a Cursillo weekend. It was not a place she expected to meet God.

> I wasn't that wild about going, because it was really emotional and there were people hugging each other. Weird.... We were near the end of the retreat and the priest said, "Well, what do you think of it so far?" And I said, "Well, it was pretty good," but no lightning had struck—and I wanted it to be this mountaintop experience. Then I somehow got to talking about being afraid of God.... And I said, "Well, if God knows absolutely everything I've ever said or done or thought of, then God wouldn't go anywhere near someone who had done what I've done." The priest said, "Why don't you admit it and pray to God that you are afraid?" There was this crucifix in this room. So I looked up at the crucifix, and I said very quietly, "God, I'm afraid to tell you who I've been and who I am"—with the

group there around me. And it hit me. I had this rush that started at my toes and went all the way up to the top of my head. This incredible heat. I just had the sense that I was filled with incredible joy and I knew then that, no matter what, God loved me totally and utterly. That so filled me and touched me and to this day is the highlight of my spiritual life. I peaked at sixteen. That sense of being loved totally and utterly has stayed with me.

To help foster a spirit of evangelism among lay leaders, Bonnie introduced Bible study at the beginning of every vestry meeting. At first, this was a stretch for vestry members. But they have continued the practice, and now everyone expects to read scripture, share personal stories relating to the scripture, and pray together before any business is conducted. "We, a bunch of Episcopalians, have learned how to pray out loud for each other—in this wonderful way of invoking God, inviting God, and offering God prayer and blessing and in a way that they've never done before. And to me, that's *real* God talk, that's *living* God, and God living in us. And to me, that's what theology really is."

ST. PAUL'S, MCKINNEY, TEXAS, AND
ST. PAUL'S, WACO, TEXAS

I can name a dozen people in the last year who have said to me, "I've got a friend who I'm bringing to church, and his marriage is falling apart, and he's feeling a bit on the ropes." As a heads-up. And then they come. And then we meet them at the door, and we follow up with a call and visit, and we invite them to our more intimate Wednesday night worship and dinner. They've found a respite—a place that's safe—and you see some real organic friendships develop—friendship evangelism that is connected to somebody's pain. (Chuck Treadwell)

People do not always learn evangelism as a spiritual practice just because clergy or lay leaders make it an explicit focus. In some churches people embrace a spirit of evangelism simply as a result of the process of living open Christian fellowship with one another. Chuck Treadwell has found this true in the two congregations he has most recently served: St. Peter's in McKinney, Texas, and St. Paul's in Waco, Texas. Chuck describes himself as someone who didn't focus very directly on evangelism: "It's been much more organic—a slow, steady, perpetual movement, trying to build a place where people could talk about things that were important to them, where people knew who they were, cared who they were, and heard the good news." By helping people create such a place, Chuck has had the privilege of watching St. Peter's during McKinney's period of rapid growth increase in attendance over eleven years from 130 to over 400, and St. Paul's in a less rapidly growing community increase from 300 to over 360 in two years.

"Our core strategy has been to create an environment that is safe for relationships and for asking the hard questions." When people experienced such an environment, they told others about what they found. And they learned new ways of creating space for one another—and for the stranger in their midst. This was not the result of Chuck and other leaders in the church following an intentional program. "I've tried to provide an environment where other relationships can grow, but not necessarily in a systematic way. I haven't been successful in introducing the small group model into these two one-hundred-year-old churches I've served. If I were planting a church, I'd use small groups immediately. But these communities already had small groups (for instance, choir, social ministry, men's and women's groups)."

Instead, Chuck worked on transforming people's interests, helping shift each group's attention outward beyond itself. "What we do is leadership training with group leaders and teachers about how to make a class or group into a ministry. It's the obvious stuff: have something that makes people feel welcome (for instance, coffee and light snacks), intentionally welcome new people verbally and learn their names, and then offer space in each group or class for people to talk a little bit about what's going on in their lives."

The thing you hear the most from people who come to St. Peter's and stay is that they had a wonderful warm feeling when they came in. They felt that there's a lot of love there, a lot of openness, a lot of acceptance of bringing people in. There's just a warmth.... It's just a wonderful environment. — *John Burley, member*

People at St. Peter's and St. Paul's have learned to welcome the stranger into what has become an easy and natural pattern of sharing stories with one another. In the Faith and Family class at St. Paul's, which brings together parents with children ages birth to thirteen, parents have dug into difficult topics on strengthening marriages, raising children, and caring for parents—and the most important work has happened through honest discussion of real life with one another. "A lot of sharing goes on in that class, so it gets deep and honest pretty quickly." Likewise, couples and families in the church have agreed to become "mentor families," connecting with new people who are in a similar place in their lives.

Chuck acknowledged the difficulty of creating an "intimate, trusting community with an open door." But in each of these churches, Chuck successfully nurtured a consistent expectation that the church be a welcoming place, and he has empowered each congregation member to welcome others. "I model this kind of welcome by being ridiculously warm and effusive. It seems that a lot of people, including clergy, get anxious about this. But I invite people to make mistakes. I'll introduce people in line to each other and say, 'Go have a cup of coffee and say hi to each other.'" This sense of lightheartedness has provided people a way through their anxieties about inviting the stranger into conversation. Chuck described the ministry of welcome in both parishes as spacious, opening many doors and interpersonal connections without becoming invasive or demanding.

An open and spacious welcome, combined with an openness of sharing stories of pilgrimage in the life of grace, has created in each church a sense of refuge and breathing room that has allowed for healing of all kinds of wounds, even religious wounds. "One thing the Episcopal Church offers evangelically is that we're a welcoming place for people who have had very bad experiences with religion—I've talked to hundreds of people who have shared horror stories of what some pastor or priest or teacher did to them or said to them."

Like many congregations across the country, members of St. Peter's and St. Paul's have struggled to come to terms with the battles over various issues in the Episcopal Church. But Chuck has consistently invited people to keep focused on living the gospel. "How you engage the political dynamics of our denomination and the local parish has a huge impact on evangelism and church growth. We keep redirecting people by offering a clear vision of Christian life, a clear sense of purpose for our community, and an incredibly positive focus. I believe this kind of focus can be truly powerful in conservative and liberal congregations alike."

Chuck acknowledged that church leaders do not always set such a tone, to the detriment of a congregation's spiritual vitality. "I know a congregation that is losing members in droves—a conservative priest came there who has not found a way to be positive, and pours out nega-

Our identity should/must/has to hang on Jesus Christ

tivity, and it's just poison. This happens in liberal congregations, too. Our congregation's clarity of purpose involves reaching people for Christ, telling the story of Jesus, bringing people into a living relationship with Jesus, and helping people connect with others and build relationships to support their relationships with God and reach out in love to the world. But we haven't hung our identity on a theological opinion about this or that—we've hung our identity on Jesus Christ and bringing people into a shared relationship."

St. Peter's and St. Paul's have not merely become focused on warmth and intimacy for their own sake; they have focused their journeys together on Jesus Christ and the life of grace. For Chuck, preaching and worship have been primary ways of setting this tone, through directness, relevance, and energy. "I'm not a biblical fundamentalist," he explains, "but I do have an almost exclusive focus on the gospel in the pulpit—really telling the stories of Jesus. I actually do expository preaching, where I ask people to open their Bibles. The first time I did that here, I told people to dust off the pew Bibles, and people laughed, because there really was dust on the spines of the pew Bibles. I take my work in the pulpit as Christianity 101 every week—I take nothing for granted. And then, it's connecting the stories week to week: 'Last week we talked about this, and two weeks ago we talked about this.'"

Through preaching that connects themes and stories week after week, Chuck has invited people into the Great Story of God's redemptive work in Jesus, and has helped them connect this story directly with the unfolding stories of their own lives. The liturgy then offers a means of expressing gratitude and wonder at God's abundant love, with children as well as adults participating in that expression directly. He notes:

> Liturgy also needs to be energized—this doesn't necessarily mean that you need pull-down screens

and projectors and "me-and-Jesus" pop-tunes. But people DO respond to energy, so the pop-tunes can be really helpful in some places. But we've never gone that direction in the congregations I've worked with. At St. Peter's, worship was just electric: McKinney was an epicenter of young families and the fastest growing county in the United States, so part of it was the children. In both churches, the liturgy still brings people in, and that's what people talk to others about—people talk about how it's alive and beautiful and energized—even in a formal setting, it's a tender experience.

♦　♦　♦　♦　♦

These are just a few snapshots of evangelism—and there are so many other stories to be told. Individuals and communities in the Episcopal Church have found many creative ways of proclaiming good news to others, journeying with others as fellow pilgrims, learning the language of others in order to speak of God's grace, naming the Holy in others' lives, and inviting others into a community of faithful sojourners. In these vitalized communities, people speak with delight to their friends and neighbors about their experiences of wonder and gratitude, honor the image of God in the searching souls of their friends, and invite them to come along and explore God's abundant love. Yes, the ministries, programs, sermons, music, and liturgies of the church can become their own vehicles of evangelism. But they only serve to complete the evangelistic circle when people encounter them through meaningful relationships that involve the sharing of stories among fellow pilgrims.

chapter four

With Open and Courageous Hearts

Tools for Evangelism

If I speak in the tongues of mortals and of angels, but do not have love, I am a noisy gong or clanging cymbal.

(1 Corinthians 13:1)

How do we go about the work of transforming our ideas about evangelism and creating an effective spiritual practice of evangelism? Let us begin with Paul's words to the Christians in Corinth, words that remind us we don't have to be extraverts in order to be effective evangelists. St. Paul's words in his first letter to the Corinthians are about *motivation*—and about people's ability to see through our words to our motivations. People are smarter than we give them credit for. They can often sense when they are being manipulated, conned, or fed an empty performance—and for young people, this is particularly true in their encounters with religion. Conversely, people also know when they are hearing the voice of genuine love, heartfelt honesty, or courageous vulnerability. These are our first tools for effective evangelism: the ability to speak and act with love, honesty, and courage about God's transforming power in our lives. The more we learn to love without embarrassment, to tell the truth to ourselves and one another, and to speak and act in spite of our fears, the more we will become living testaments to God's redeeming work. Evangelism begins with prayer for the Holy Spirit to transform us and teach us these things.

Now, there are more than a few "strategies" and "tools" that won't work—that are turn-offs because they communicate something other than genuine love and joy. Just try these "sure-fire strategies to turn people off" and see how they work for you:

1) Come to our church—we NEED you!

2) See how slick and polished we are.

3) Try Christ—you really need *something.*

4) Come to my church, so that someone else can tell you the story I'm too timid to tell myself.

5) Yeah, I'm not sure how much of all of this I believe myself—but come anyway.

Besides an overemphasis on getting people "in the door" and thus focusing on the institution, these strategies come across as insulting and fail to communicate the deep integrity, beauty, and truth of our own stories of transformation by God's grace.

Too frequently, I have heard and watched Christians rely on the institution through its worship, fellowship, and preaching—or even on the fact that it exists—to tell the stories of transformation that others are ready to hear but that they are too timid or uncertain to share themselves. This *laissez-faire* approach to evangelism reminds me of two stories. One is from the television show "The Simpsons." Ned Flanders, a tightly wound religious soul, as a rowdy child is taken to a psychiatrist by his "lousy beatnik parents." His parents are heard to say, "You've gotta help us, doc. We've tried nothing, and we're all out of ideas." The other story is from a parish I served. When we were considering ways to become a more hospitable place, the congregation was considering new and improved signs and directions in the church building—including signs to the bathroom. Lizzie, an outspoken member who was not particularly happy with some of these changes, said, "Why do we need signs telling people where the bathrooms are? They can always ask someone, can't they?"

---

inner transformation: the first step in evangelism

Without inner change, no tools or methods for evangelism will ring true—we will simply be noisy gongs or clanging cymbals. As with the development of any spiritual practices, transformation of behavior begins with a focus on inner transformation. What kinds of inner transformation will prepare us for a profound spiritual practice of evangelism? There are many possibilities we can consider—but here are six.

1) *Self-love.* As Christians, we are seeking and learning to love ourselves as Christ loves us, both our unlovely and lovely parts. We can practice self-love in a waking prayer each morning: "I love you, God, for my being." We can also allow ourselves to be loved by others through times of celebration, mourning, and forgiveness, and when we discover love by loving others.

2) *Self-knowledge.* In ongoing transformation, we develop habits of recognizing and voicing our ultimate need for God and for rigorous but loving self-examination. We have

Spiritual Reflection is very important

brief opportunities to do this kind of self-examination every week in our confession of sin during the Sunday Eucharist. Clergy can invite the people gathered to reflect more directly on their lives during the silence before confession, and give more space for honest self-reflection. We can also take part in the Prayer Book rite of reconciliation, where we share our confession with another person, lay or ordained. This kind of honesty with ourselves is attractive to people who have not yet dared to admit to themselves who they are or explore who they are becoming.

Churches strengthening self-knowledge
Churches can help Christians learn more clearly who they are through focus discipleship experiences such as EFM (Education for Ministry), DOCC (Disciples of Christ in Community), Alpha, Via Media, Faith Alive, and Cursillo.

3) *Compassion.* Compassion is not pity, but the recognition of another person's full humanity, warts and all. Self-knowledge leads us to compassion through prayerful reflection on our own fallible, fragile, and fleeting lives, and how all benefits in our lives depend on the contributions of many people.

Churches strengthening compassion
Outreach ministries help members develop and strengthen their sense of compassion, such as Stephen Ministries, Night Ministry, Habitat for Humanity, Oxfam and the Heifer Project, mission trips and projects, local outreach and advocacy, community organizing, and the Millennium Development Goals.

Parishes can assist in fostering compassion by offering outreach programs that employ an action-reflection model, in which people do work (like building a house for Habitat for Humanity) and then return to discuss why they did what they did and what they learned. Parishes can also create an environment of honest encounter with local and international human needs, through periodic videos and invited speakers.

4) *Courage.* Courage, or fortitude, helps us to overcome anxiety and become eager to proclaim the source of our strength and joy. Courage does not mean becoming a bully. Nonviolent protest demands courage to walk or stand in the place of the enemy. Assertiveness demands courage to say what you mean and to speak directly to error. Vulnerability to tell one's own story demands courage. These are habits that congregations can foster. Clergy and laity alike can practice courage in how they engage conflict and speak the truth about their experiences with one another.

Churches strengthening courage
Churches can help people strengthen their courage by sending individuals and teams on missions, holding table gatherings where people are invited and expected to speak their minds (as modeled at General Convention 2000), creating partnerships with agencies to offer anxiety-reduction and assertiveness training, and participating in youth programs like Outward Bound.

5) *Integrity.* At the close of the Eucharist, we pray for "gladness and *singleness* of heart." Unfortunately, we find it all too easy to live compartmentalized and divided lives, splitting off our religious life from the rest of our lives.

Churches strengthening integrity
Churches can help foster and strengthen lives of integrity by encouraging participation in Twelve-Step programs, parish-wide daily prayer practice ("We pledge to pray the noonday office every day at work, school, home, or on the road."), and programs supporting faithful habits in family life.

The popularity of the "WWJD—What Would Jesus Do?" bracelets is simply an expression of a prayer for integrity, for singleness of heart focused on living as Jesus would have us live. And we need not enter this work alone—dedicated small groups help hold us accountable and focus on our single-hearted purpose to live as disciples.

6) *Humility.* Humility emerges with increased self-knowledge and compassion—and it provides a safeguard against false self-love and overly aggressive "courage." True humility involves a recognition that I speak, act, and live as one life, one person with limited but real experiences and perspectives to share in these fleeting moments—and that my unique life does not give me more privilege of voice and action than anyone else. The Amish understand this particularly well in their emphasis on foot-washing as what an outsider might dare to call a sacramental act. Foot-washing, like the exchange of the Peace, is one of the great leveling actions in the church, where each of us is servant, and each of us is served—and both positions take humility.

It is important to note that communities committed to the kind of discipleship that involves these six inner transformations will naturally strengthen their practices of continuing evangelism, as they apply themselves to teaching and training their children in living the Christian faith. "Primary evangelism" will emerge naturally—churches committed to ongoing transformation in the Spirit are going to attract people. Changed lives speak.

Below are a series of questions for exploration by individuals, small groups, and congregations. These questions invite you into loving self-assessment by asking you to identify moments in your life in which you have been learning or experiencing self-love, increased self-knowledge, compassion, courage, integrity, and humility. The questions are meant to open the door to self-reflection, prayer, and the sharing of stories with one another.

SELF-LOVE

- Name a time that you knew you loved yourself. What happened? What did you love?
- When have you been deeply grateful for being you, for your life, for your experiences?
- What do you hold dear about yourself? What do you not love about yourself?
- What does God love in you that you do not yet love? How can you ask the Holy Spirit to be in conversation with that part of yourself?

SELF-KNOWLEDGE

- When have you seen something about yourself you hadn't seen before? How did you take in that new information?
- In the course of your life, what new has emerged, what has died, and what has remained constant?
- What are your "favorite" or habitual sins—done and left undone?

COMPASSION

- Who is an example of compassion for you?
- When has your heart stirred with an expansive love and desire to commit yourself to the good of others? What sparked that experience, and what did you do?
- Whom do you love most dearly and whom do you despise? Where are each of them hurting or vulnerable in their lives? Can you hold them and their vulnerability in your heart with compassion?

COURAGE

- Who is an example of courage for you?
- When have you faced and overcome anxiety in speaking the truth or acting according to your deepest convictions?

- When have you stood up to somebody for destructive behavior?

INTEGRITY
- Who is an example of integrity for you?
- When have you acted with the greatest integrity?
- Have you ever felt divided against yourself, acting or speaking in ways out of keeping with your deepest convictions?
- Who is good at "holding your feet to the fire"?

HUMILITY
- Who have been important examples of humility for you, in history and your own life?
- When have you made a contribution to people's lives and been the least concerned about recognition for your contributions or skills?
- Who helps keep you humble, in the best sense of the word? What does that person do to help bring you back to a different sense of yourself?
- What does it mean to you that Christ "emptied himself" to live and die among us?

---

habits for evangelism

PRACTICING GRATITUDE

Gratitude is the fundamental act of worship. Whether in everyday mundane exchanges with others or in our most central act together—celebrating the Eucharist, which means "thanksgiving"—our expressions of gratitude are moments of worship and adoration. As we give ourselves freely to expressing our wonder at the wideness in God's mercies, our lives are transformed into sacraments of thanksgiving for the goodness of the Lord.

Ignatian examen ✓

The practice of gratitude is not blind optimism, but a mental choice we make. There are famous classroom studies—and more recent studies in business—that have demonstrated the "Pygmalion effect": when a teacher assumes that a child will do well, the teacher treats the child differently, offering more challenges and rewarding performance more vigorously—and the child responds by rising to the occasion. Our practice of gratitude with others helps others see themselves differently. People experience us reflecting back to them that we have witnessed the image of God within them.

To foster habits of gratitude and wonder, individuals and groups alike can use a modified form of the Ignatian *examen*—a review of each day in conversation with God. Toward the closing of each day, review with God the gifts you received and the joys you experienced. These gifts may be as seemingly insignificant as a smile from a friend or stranger, good basic customer service at a store, an extra hug from your child or a chore done without complaint, a kiss from a lover, or even the trains running on time and the trash getting picked up. Or they may be more extraordinary, like a moment of reconciliation with an estranged family member, an unexpected inheritance, a gift from your parents that clearly indicates their personal sacrifice, or forgiveness from someone from whom you least expected it. Recall whether or not you remembered to express your gratitude in the moment, to yourself, to God, and to the other person. Ask God for guidance and clarity in such moments in the future. The next day, be mindful of choosing at least one situation in which you will be intentional about expressing gratitude directly, in the moment, to another person and to God. This is of course a personal practice, but it can be done in small groups as well—and it works particularly well in families, as a part of the Faith Stepping Stones approach to helping families form habits of faithful Christian practices in their children.

Great spiritual practice

Congregations can learn the habit of gratitude through exchanges of gifts and thanksgiving with one another and their surrounding communities. When clergy and lay leaders start saying "thank you" through notes, emails, and phone calls, they often learn that this is the first time some people have ever been thanked for their labors in church. A neglect of gratitude shifts the spirit of congregational life from gift to duty, from possible source of joy to necessity. How simply we can begin to transform our common life by expressing gratitude to one another. This can extend to gratitude for people in our surrounding communities who help sustain our common life. Imagine how a community might respond to a church that held services, festivals, or dinner celebrations for people who work in all sectors of labor and public service!

It is also possible to help people recognize in everyday life their own moments of deep gratitude. I recently met with a young couple for marital counseling. Neither was connected to the church, but when I asked them how they talked and connected with one another on spiritual matters, Stan perked up and talked about a time in the past week when they were out to dinner. He had shared with Sharon how the moment struck him—that he was amazed and grateful that they were able to enjoy such a pleasure as a sharing a meal at a restaurant where they could eat outside in a beautiful environment, and remembering that so many people do not have access to the same delights. We discussed this moment as a way they had already prayed together, and that this was actually a prayer of gratitude— their "grace" over a meal. They responded with surprise and delight, and agreed to continue these conversations with each other.

We tend to be most anxious about different kinds of rejection, not knowing what to say, being tested about our faith, and coming off like a fanatic.

◆ Don't get hung up on the fact that they might say "no" — remind yourself that you are only responsible for proclaiming good news, not for other people's responses.

◆ Don't get hung up about doing it right—remember Jesus' sower, who dropped seeds willy-nilly everywhere— seeds are small but plentiful, and they end up everywhere.

◆ Don't take yourself so seriously! Seeing the humor in evangelism is a sign of healthy humility. People look pretty ridiculous during sex, but they seem to look forward to it and enjoy themselves anyway. Can it be much worse living lives of gratitude and wonder?

◆ Don't worry about being able to defend your faith flawlessly, even when you are asked difficult questions by people close to you, including your own children, siblings, or parents. Review with your sisters and brothers in Christ why you believe and live as you do, and think about how your own experience of God relates to Christian beliefs.

◆ "Sin boldly"! The only way to learn to tell your stories of good news is to tell them; the only way to name the Holy in others is to name it. There is adventure in the risk.

◆ Remember it is highly unlikely that you will look or act anything like a "Jesus freak."

LEARNING TO LISTEN

Developing awareness begins with curiosity about the people around us—both in our individual lives and in our shared congregational life. We begin to pay attention to those in our neighborhood, on the streets, in the stores and malls, among our colleagues at work and school, in the parks, on the playgrounds, and in the clubs and gyms. Like the man in Luke's gospel who wants to inherit eternal life, we begin to ask Jesus, "Who is my neighbor?" (Luke 10:29). As we become more practiced in compassion and gratitude in our everyday lives, we will encounter other people differently—and begin to notice more acutely our own internal barriers in interacting with people who are not like us.

Thus, the next step in effective evangelism is learning to listen. "Evangelistic listening" is deep and respectful listening to the life stories of others and seeking out signs of the presence and work of the Holy Spirit. But it begins with listening to the everyday concerns, experiences, and perspectives of people around you. Evangelism and church growth writers frequently stress the importance of getting to know census data and other sources of information on population trends and other changes in their communities. I agree. There are many such resources that can help a congregation get a better picture of the needs, interests, passions, and changes in its surrounding communities. Sometimes, congregations experience such reflection on "the big picture" as an awakening and a challenge to their sense of relevance and importance in the community.

Data Resources about Your Community
+ *U.S. Census*: search by zip code, city, or census tract (www.census.gov)
+ *Percept*: fee-for-service analysis of the area surrounding a church, both demographics and attitudes (www.percept.org)
+ *InfoUSA*: white pages database for the entire country; can provide data searches by age, income, etc. (www.infousa.com)
+ *Town or city hall websites*: document neighborhood changes and developments

---

These kinds of data are only introductions, however, and no substitute for good, honest footwork. You will need to get out and "pound the pavement," visiting shops, parks, coffeehouses, bars, libraries, and neighborhoods, striking up conversations with strangers, and getting to know them and their experiences in the community. This kind of work is integral to learning the practice of a kind of "holy curiosity" about our neighbors and daring to get to know them. It is the only way we begin to enter the work of the incarnate Christ, who "pitched a tent" among us. Truly radical hospitality begins here, with a non-defensive willingness to hear anything, including judgments against God, religion, and church—even yours.

When I am exploring a neighborhood or getting to know my neighbors or new colleagues, I ask questions like the following:

* Where are you from, and what brought you here? Why did you decide to live/work here? What kind of life do you want to have here, for yourself and your family?

* What's your overall impression of this town or neighborhood? What kinds of folks live/work here?

* What would you like to see happen in this community? What is happening here that concerns you? What excites you? What are some issues that are really important to you?

* What are your favorite spots here? Where do you like to spend time?

* What are some things you can do that you like to share with others or offer others?

* Who do you turn to when you need help? Who do you rely on?

* What are the best things about this place? What are some things that concern you?

These and other open-ended questions allow people to respond with stories that give you glimpses of their ideals, yearnings, needs, and passions.

Community organizers rely on this kind of listening to understand the needs, interests, and strengths of a community, and to help bring people together in networks of common goals. Training organizations like the Industrial Areas Foundation, Gamaliel, and People Invested in Community Organizing teach community organizers how to do "one-on-one's"—conversations with people in their homes and places of work, where they can use their powers of observation to identify what might be core concerns and interests of people. Many pastors and lay people who have gone through this training for their congregations have found their whole way of understanding ministry transformed. Perhaps a picture of a graduating teenager or a book about Mexico on a shelf says something about what is important to a person you are visiting. What can you ask about it?

Community Organizing Training for Congregational Leaders and Teams: Each of these major community organizing networks has a distinctive approach, but all emphasize the importance of faith communities in strengthening communities and citizens.

+ *Industrial Areas Foundation* (www.industrialareasfoundation.org/)
+ *Gamaliel Foundation* (www.gamaliel.org/)
+ *PICO Network* (www.piconetwork.org/)
+ *ACORN* (www.acorn.org/)

"Evangelistic listening" does not mean asking *religious* questions. Those can come later. "Evangelistic listening" means listening for the spiritual and theological meaning in what people are telling you about their experiences in your community. When a mother tells you she is worried about bullies on the playground, what are her heartfelt spiritual concerns? What is spiritually important in the story a contractor who tells of having to fire some day-laborers who were making too many mistakes on the job? When people talk about their community as safe or unsafe, beautiful or run down, healthy or unhealthy, are they saying anything deeper about what they are seeking in life and what they believe is right and good?

Questions for "Evangelistic Listening"

1. What do you love most about your life—right now? Why?

2. What do you hate most about your life—right now? Why?

3. What books, movies, events, or people have really had an impact on your life? How?

4. When have you felt really connected to the human race, the world, the universe, or some large group greater than yourself? When have you felt really alone?

5. Say something bad—terrible—happens in your life, or to someone you know. How do you understand or make sense of life when things are not going well?

6. What takes the most out of you? What takes the least out of you?

7. Think for a minute about the world as you know it. How do you make sense of the world? What kind of a place is the world, in general, to you?

8. How do you fit into the world? What do you see as your place in the world?

9. Is there a principle by which you try to live your life? How did you come to believe that?

10. Who are the people or groups that help lift your spirits?

It is not difficult to invite people into conversations about their beliefs and values—and it is possible to do this without using "God-language." In my research and work with young adults, I developed a range of questions that allowed them to talk to me about their personal theologies—their beliefs and values about the world, human purpose, and cosmic justice. I have found that I can use

Naming the holy in our lives is key to evangelism.

these questions with anyone from adolescence through old age, as I seek to understand the soulful concerns of a community and its people.

NAMING THE HOLY IN YOUR LIFE

Now we are to the heart of evangelism. The essential step in becoming an effective evangelist is learning to name the Holy, being comfortable naming the moments in our lives when God was most clearly evident to us. We can do this by taking stock of our lives, recalling moments of discovery or new opportunity, difficulty or trauma, celebration, sadness and loss, fear, surprise, profound friendship or solitude, or simply peace and contentment. We can do this by recalling important events, amazing places, and influential people in our lives. And, as we might find it difficult to recall these moments readily, we can help ourselves remember by asking ourselves the same questions we will use with others in spiritual and theological conversations.

But before we can *tell* our own stories, we must come to *know* our own stories. This means that we have to pay attention to our lives as they are unfolding every day, and review the events that have touched us and stayed with us in our personal histories. The "spiritual timeline" can be a powerful way to review our lives and put together our stories in new and surprising ways. Education for Ministry (EFM) and Disciples of Christ in Community (DOCC) programs use the "spiritual timeline" in a way similar to the following:

1) Take a piece of paper, turn it sideways (or put several papers side-by-side), and draw a horizontal line across the middle, marking off years of your life in even increments (every three, five, or ten years) starting from birth.

2) Using one color, mark the "highs" (above the horizontal line) and "lows" (below the horizontal line) that you remember happening at different points in your life—"external" events and experiences when you were surprised by delight, changed, stuck in a rut, or dismayed by loss (such as births, deaths, changes in job, health, and relationships).

3) Using a different color, mark the "highs" and "lows" of your spiritual life—times of closeness to and distance from God, inner turmoil and transformation, meaning and belonging and purpose (or their absence). These may or may not involve church.

4) Tell the story you have drawn on your "spiritual timeline" to others in a small group. Each story will take time—allow twenty to thirty minutes. Clearly highlight moments in your life when you sensed God at work. Others in the group listen prayerfully, offering thoughts after you finish on how they sensed God at work in your life story.

Obviously, this exercise from EFM and DOCC is meant to be done in small groups, and will take several meetings together to complete all the stories. But the first three steps of this exercise can be done in solitude as well, as a way of holding one's life before God in prayer.

You may also find helpful another modified Ignatian *examen*. First, quiet yourself, and become aware of God's many graces. Reflect on the goodness of being and of being loved. Ask for clarity and openness to receive God's guidance as you review some events and experiences of your life. Note any memories that arouse powerful emotions, and hold these emotions before God, expressing gratitude, wonder, sorrow, or anger as it arises. Make note of what struck you in these moments and think prayerfully about how they shaped you.

Exercise: "O Taste and See that the Lord is Good"

In his book *Feeding the Flock: Restaurants and Churches You'd Stand in Line For,* Russell Chandler raises two interesting questions: What is it about some restaurants that they end up attracting standing-room-only crowds? And why does that happen with some churches? Common to both was the power of word-of-mouth testimony. One of the best questions raised by this book is how easy it is for us to share our joy about a wonderful restaurant. We find it similarly easy to describe with gusto our favorite concerts, movies, and vacation destinations.

Find someone with whom to do this exercise.

1) Tell the other person about an amazing meal you had (or concert, movie, sports game, or place in nature). Talk about what that meal was like, what you experienced, and what it did for you. Get into the details!

◆ What was it like, telling someone that story?

2) Now, think about a moment when you have feasted on God's goodness (or reveled in life's unfolding drama, music, or energy). Tell the other person about that moment—what happened, what the experience meant to you, and how God met you in that experience.

◆ How was telling that story similar to, and different from, telling the first story? Were you able to speak with the same freedom? Were you as excited? Were you anxious?

This is an exercise that can be done in groups of three—each taking turns as the storyteller, the listener, and the observer. By repeating this exercise with the same people, and with different people, you learn how to find and tell your sacred stories more freely, how to listen more effectively, notice your own anxiety, and how to help one another become more natural bearers of—and listeners to—good news.

Coming at things from a different angle, some may find it helpful simply to talk to themselves about God. This may seem an odd suggestion. And yet, with a faith that stresses the incarnational reach of God into the gritty nature of creation itself as a habitation, talking about God should be as easy as talking about an apple, or bread, or a friend. We may simply need practice. So, talk to yourself about God. Let this conversation with yourself become a kind of prayer, where you say to yourself all that you have felt, thought, experienced, or doubted about God. And, to keep the conversation interesting, talk to God about God. We are free in prayer to speak to God directly and tell God directly what we think and feel. And, just to complete the loop, talk to God about yourself.

If we grow more accustomed to talking to ourselves about God, we will likely become more comfortable talking to others about God. Likewise, if we grow more accustomed to talking to God and asking God about ourselves, we will likely find it easier to talk to others—and to ask others—about ourselves. Which brings us, finally, to telling others our own story. When I *know* my own story, I know what I have to offer, and can present parts of my life as a living testament to the love of Christ and the surprising presence of the Holy Spirit.

YOUR MOST SACRED CHRISTIAN STORIES

Each of us has Christian stories or passages from scripture and tradition that we treasure—stories that enrich, expand, and undergird our understandings and experiences of God. We can practice telling these stories and passages to ourselves and others, and practice connecting the stories of our own lives with them. This is at the heart of Christian spirituality and witness, and is lively in many African-American and Native American Christian traditions. Your most sacred Christian stories might include tales and narratives from the Bible—the days of creation, Abraham bargaining with God, Ruth following Naomi, Nathan confronting David and David confessing, or Jesus at the wedding at Cana, teaching Nicodemus, feeding thousands of people, or healing the lepers. You may have favorite poetic passages from the Psalms or other Wisdom literature, the prophets, or the New Testament hymns to Christ. You may be stirred by stories of saints through the ages, like those of Francis of Assisi or Julian of Norwich, Dietrich Bonhoeffer or Martin Luther King, Jr., Dorothy Day or William Stringfellow. There may also be "secular" songs, stories, and movies that express for you core gospel themes of God's relationship with humanity and humanity's search for God. Many in my generation found powerful expressions of the gospel in the music of U2, the Indigo Girls, and Cake, and in movies like *The Mission, Shawshank Redemption,* and *The Matrix.*

At age two-and-a-half, my daughter Cassie had a favorite Bible story—the parable called "The Lost Sheep." When we brought her children's Bible to church or got it out to read at dinner, she asked for that story, and for "The Really Big Picnic" (the feeding of the five thousand). One day we stopped by the Sonoma Mission—the northernmost Spanish mission in California. When we went into the chapel, Cassie wanted to climb up the steps of the pulpit. I explained what the pulpit was for, but that we couldn't use it, since it was roped off. She said, "All right, I'll stand here and preach." She proceeded to tell the story of the shepherd and the lost sheep—and then continued with the story of the woman and the lost coin. She then asked me to take a turn preaching the same story.

Some biblical stories and passages have become very much *mine* in how they speak to me and for me. During a tumultuous time in graduate school, in the midst of conflict with a faculty advisor, I was worried that everything was going to collapse around me—that I would lose my research position and project, and that I would possibly not be able to continue. I came home to my apartment, sat down, and opened the Psalms. I came upon Psalm 63, and my eyes became fixed on the verse that reads, "My soul clings to you; your right hand holds me fast." I closed my eyes and began to pray that verse over and over again, breathing in and out with each phrase. I felt steadied, calmed, and re-centered. For over a year, that verse was my daily "mantra." At first, I prayed it for myself. Then I found that I could pray it for others as I encountered people throughout the day. I still return to that verse as a clear expression of my yearning for God and my hopeful trust that God will hold me.

One of my favorite phrases in our liturgies comes up only once a year, at Ash Wednesday. I remember the moment when the words "Remember that you are dust, and to dust you shall return" changed from something I anticipated with solemnity and anxiety to something I received gladly as a gift. I came to a point where I was grateful for my mortality and happy to be reminded of it. I now find myself smiling at the moment when a priest says the words to me and I feel the slightly rough rub of ashes on my forehead. I am glad that this life—for all its joys and troubles—has an end. I do not want that end to come too soon! But I am grateful that I do not bear the responsibility of more than this one life, so I can embrace the responsibility and gift of this life more fully. The Word of God speaks in new ways to me and for me as I live the fullness of my life, and I find my own story interweaving in new ways with the Great Story of God's redemptive work, reconciling presence, and passionate love relationship with humanity and all creation.

WHERE IS GOD IN YOUR NEIGHBOR'S LIFE?
Now comes that risky but wonderful practice of naming the Holy in someone else's life, bearing witness to what we perceive as the presence and work of the Holy Spirit. Admittedly this takes practice, and must always be done with humility as well as courage—for instance, "You know, Sarah, God seems to have been guiding you," or "Paul, maybe God is already having some conversations with you—what do you think?" But it is not nearly so

daunting if we have spent time and effort cultivating our other evangelistic spiritual practices by which we develop natural habits of sharing our own stories and allowing them to interweave with the great stories of Christian scripture and tradition. The more natural and easy we become at naming our own experiences of grace, the more naturally we will find ourselves naming the Holy in other people's lives—a profound, intimate gift that strengthens bonds of human affection.

It is possible that someone will reject the notion of God at work in her life, at least at first. But be alert: someone's seeming rejection may be accompanied by a quizzical look that might be asking, "Do you really mean that? Are you for real?" Don't simply withdraw your naming of the Holy—you might even gently and pleas-antly persist, suggesting once again that God may indeed be at work. As someone accepts this possibility or is at least considering it, you may be surprised by the different reactions he might have. Laughter of recognition, thoughtful silence, quiet tears, a sigh, a smile, a scowl of deep thought: all of these are responses that let you know that your gift has arrived and been opened.

We should not rush rashly into such profound space, but neither should we retreat from such encounters simply out of fear of walking on holy ground. Naming the Holy in others' lives requires discernment, courage, vulnera-bility, and deep respect—the kind of response required of Moses in response to God's invitation, "Take off your shoes, for this is holy ground."

The process of this evangelistic practice is simple, really—which does not mean that it is simplistic or easy. There are three things we do: 1) Listen; 2) Pray and adore; and 3) Speak.

Listen first. It is too easy to skip or minimize this crucial gift we offer in evangelism. When the urgency to speak strikes you, ask yourself first, "Have I truly heard?

Have I listened to the heart of this person's story?" When the temptation to give up or ignore a story hits you, ask yourself, "What am I missing?" Intent and focused listening brings us into contact with things people may not even be aware that they are saying—and lets people know that we are genuinely interested in their lives.

We listen not just with our ears, but with our eyes, our bodies, our souls. The more deeply we listen, the more we will hold up a mirror to others, allowing them to see themselves in new ways. Can you repeat the story? Did you catch the change in vocal inflection, the smile, the shift in posture? Did you follow emotions where they led? Are you able to summarize, to play as it were a short film documenting what you have seen and heard? Can you ask the questions that allow more to be revealed? These are the signs of profound listening.

In the midst of listening, questions will occur to us: *What was the turning point? How did God break through? Is this person hearing how he talks about this important moment in his life? Where are the signs of God at work in the imagination, motivations, feelings, and actions of the people involved?* These questions can become our prayers, that the Holy Spirit open our eyes to see Christ at work. When we recognize the marks of God in someone's story, then we may dare to name the Holy: "Jan, I believe you met God in that moment." "Jason, God is at work in your life—can you feel it?" "Thank you, Sarah—you have shown me Christ." This is by no means a casual or tentative statement; it is a moment of profound but simple worship and proclamation.

Families are a natural first place to practice. Imagine how different our interactions with teenagers—and with parents—would be if we entered such conversation with one another at least once a week, inviting Holy stories and being prepared to name the Holy in each other. We can model this for our families and guests at various gatherings, like holidays, cookouts, and receptions. And, as so many families find themselves getting locked into patterns of seeing and naming only the negative in one another—or in taking one another for granted—there is a great ministry for us to embrace, to offer ourselves as "surrogate" grandparents, children, and family members who will speak words of wonder, joy, and adoration.

Once you have offered this gift to someone, allow the person some time and space to respond. It may also be helpful to offer a piece of your own story, or a story from scripture or Christian tradition, to help someone through this powerful and vulnerable experience. It is a good idea to ask permission to share your own story or something from scripture. "May I share something that your story reminded me of?" It may help someone to connect the dots and see something new and unexpected in her own life.

Congregations can engage more explicitly in naming the Holy by marking and honoring major transitions in people's lives. Such transitions include those traditionally marked in church rites—baptism, marriage, and burial—where opportunities for naming the Holy extend well before and after one liturgy or prayer. But there is a host of other transitions in life that can be marked by times of public prayer, blessing, and acknowledgment of change: graduations, relocations and moves, job changes, and retirements are all worthy of community prayer and recognition. Other significant transitions, such as births, engagements and marriages, and deaths, afford multiple opportunities *beyond* church rites and liturgies for the community to name the Holy and bless the people involved.

The preparation is done. We are forming new habits and practices with our faith and discovering the wonder and delight of hearing and telling the stories. Now comes that next major step: Stepping out from our safe enclave, becoming the pilgrims we really are, and bringing our stories of gratitude and wonder into our day-to-day inter-actions with people. Now is not a time to return to fear and anxiety. Now we must remember our practice of allowing ourselves to be in the grip of gratitude—for it is our gratitude that propels us out to a waiting world.

God goes before us. "Grandmother" Kaze Gadaway offers advice on how to help people develop this awareness as a habit: "One exercise I had the young people do was to go out onto the streets of Holbrook and look around—and ask, 'Where is God here?' And, you know, they found God in all sorts of places. Once they had done this the first time, they were excited to do it again. So I sent them home with the same question to ask through the week."

Beginning with "Grandmother" Kaze's lead, it is a simple matter to begin talking to people we meet, inviting them into conversation and inviting them to talk about themselves. Most people experience our interest and curiosity as a gift—and, while they may be initially surprised by questions that invite them to share important life experiences, most respond gladly to this opportunity to talk about things they usually don't get a chance to share. It can be helpful to remember some of the "evangel-istic questions" outlined earlier in this chapter, to help focus our conversations. If we can allow ourselves to respond to the lure of God that tugs us out into our communities, fuelled by our gratitude and excitement of discovery, God will become as much a natural part of our public and private discourse as food, and we will need no more gimmicks or buttons or tracts or catch phrases.

Exercise: Where is God Here?

This exercise is best done in small groups—but it can also be done in pairs, or even alone with a journal.

Step 1: Go out onto the streets surrounding your church. As you walk, prayerfully ask, "Where is God here?" Pay attention, and note what you discover. Come back after 45 minutes and report to your group (or partner or journal).

Step 2: Go out onto the streets surrounding your home, school, or workplace, and ask the same question. Pay attention, note what you discover, and come back a week later and report to your group.

Step 3: Go out from your church and this time talk to someone. Listen to his or her story. Come back after 45 minutes. Tell the group what you heard, and ask for the group's insights—helping you name the Holy and thinking about how to respond.

Step 4: Go out from your home, school, or workplace, and talk to someone. Come back the next week to your group, share what you heard, and ask for insights and input.

Step 5: Go out from your church, talk to someone, listen to his or her story, and this time offer a response—naming the Holy in his or her experience. Tell a story of your own. Come back to the group and discuss your experience.

Step 6: Go out from your home, school, or workplace, invite someone's story, and offer your response, naming the Holy and sharing something from yourself, scripture, or Christian tradition. Come back to the group and discuss what you experienced.

In our neighborhoods, we can engage in regular periods of "coffeehouse conversations": small groups from congregations can spread out in a community, going to coffeehouses, parks, clubs, and bars and can begin conversations with people through the practice of evangelistic listening. Young people may be able to help us relearn the freedom of speaking naturally about our faith in the midst of everyday conversation. Instant messaging, email, and website conversation spaces like MySpace and Facebook have allowed people to find new freedom with each other in conversation. With the power of partial anonymity, people talk about themselves with surprising openness. Religion and faith enter conversations alongside food, music, relationships, and work. A few years ago, I was playing backgammon online. My opponent was a single mom in Pennsylvania. Between taking our turns, we chatted—and I started talking about my involvement in church. She started asking me questions—and she trounced me in backgammon because I kept forgetting to take my turn while I was thinking about how to respond to her!

Regular practice within "coffeehouse conversations" will reveal new ministry opportunities and help the congregation connect more deeply with its surrounding community. My seminary students get the same assignment every year: to go out and talk with individuals they do not know, practicing evangelistic listening, and to bring back to the class what they learned. One student had this to say about it:

> On the day we went to do our interviews, the whole way into the city, David, we were cursing your name! I mean, we really didn't want to do this. And then, when we got to the street corner where we were going to go our separate ways to do interviews, we stopped and prayed, "Oh, Holy Spirit, help us!" And, we went and did the interviews— and we were, each one of us, transformed. We were stunned at how much people were willing to share.

With practice—and only with practice—anxiety gives way to anticipation and enjoyment. When we become this comfortable in our own "Christian skin," we will find ourselves face to face with people in moments that call for our full proclamation of the gospel. Such moments may come after many conversations and shared activities or they may come quite suddenly, at the outset of a conversation or in a situation calling for intervention. While we can never prepare fully for such moments, we can remind ourselves of what it means to care so much about the gospel that we cannot wait to sell it, share it, or give it away. We can thank God for our passions and excitement that help us let others know what we care about and want to share with them, asking for the Holy Spirit's clear voice to ring out from within us as we seek to proclaim good news to a hungry and thirsty world.

"come and see": inviting and following up

Our evangelism culminates with an explicit invitation—to come with us on a journey, to learn and experience more on the Way, to seek God with others who are seeking. As pilgrims we tell people of the places where we have found Christ, and we invite them to join us. When this moment of invitation comes, we want our faith communities to be prepared to respond effectively with its full roster of fellowship, programs, ministries, worship, and proclamation.

The practice of invitation is a spiritual discipline that involves all members of the faith community. When inviting others to "come and see," we want our invitation to be warm and clear, our welcome to be genuine and hearty, and our follow-up to communicate our gratitude and fond remembrance. There are some basic principles that can strengthen congregational practices of invitation, hospitality, and follow-up. These principles have been used by various churches, and are core guidelines in church planting, programs like Theology on Tap, and congregational development:

• *Four points of contact.* According to market researchers, people need to see or hear an announcement at least four times before responding to it, and ideally in four different ways (such as personal contact, flyer, postcard, email, advertisement). Multiple ways of announcing and inviting give you the advantages of breadth and repetition.

• *From the familiar to the unfamiliar.* The best word-of-mouth approaches emphasize starting with people you know and contexts you inhabit, and moving out from there to less familiar people and settings.

• *From personal to impersonal.* Personal contact sticks with someone longer, so the personal invitation is always best. If you are going to use multiple points of contact, lead with personal contact. Face to face is stronger than a phone call, which is more personal than a written note (but not if you leave a message!), which is more personal than email. The impersonal contacts of mass mailings, radio spots, print ads, flyers, street banners, and website postings still reach some people, but the personal invitation needs to take the lead.

• *The 1:4 ratio.* In the Theology on Tap model, each young adult who serves on any parish's planning team commits to inviting four people who typically don't go to church.[22] This is a great model: a successful evangelistic event depends on the invitational work of its planners, and by following the 1:4 ratio, a planning group ensures that the event will be well-attended (a planning group of five, for example, can expect at least twenty to twenty-five people total). It clearly gives people who are planning or creating an event the responsibility and opportunity to invite friends and neighbors. It also guarantees that the people who are invited will know at least one person when they arrive. And it keeps the focus on people who are new rather than on church "regulars."

• *Crying out in the marketplace.* A different but powerful approach is that of "Grandmother" Kaze with Navajo and white youth in Arizona, Bonnie Perry in Chicago, and students from The Office at SUNY-Buffalo. These evangelists met people directly in homes and on the streets, boldly announcing what they were there for, and being insistent and persistent in the face of initial opposition or suspicion. When you have something really good to offer, there may be times to blast it openly in public.

• *Clear directions and signs.* When I arrive somewhere, I like to see well-marked signs for parking, room locations, and restrooms—what adult wants to have to ask where the bathroom is? I also like to know that there are clearly identifiable people I can ask for help.

• *Multiple introductions.* People generally respond well to meeting more than one person at a new place. As Chuck Treadwell practices in McKinney, Texas, we can think about who we would like our invited guests to meet. Who has some common interests or experiences? When we introduce our guests to four or five people, we think about points of connection.

• *Clear self-description.* Congregations that are clearer about who they are and what they do uniquely as disciples are more likely to have a sense of vitality and energy. This clarity is also attractive to people—people like to make informed decisions about groups with which they associate. Part of being hospitable is being clear about who you are as a community.

♦ *"Improbable conversations."* John Dreibelbis, my colleague at Seabury, watched in congregations for how often people who might not usually connect found each other and engaged in conversation. Are older people talking with teenagers, and vice versa? Are people of different races or economic status talking together? The more freely people talk with each other in a community across obvious categories, the more a stranger will be intrigued and be able to imagine a place for himself.

very true at St. Martha's

♦ *Invitation to give.* Not everyone is drawn first to a community because of what they receive; sometimes it is more important for someone to sense that they have something to give, to contribute to the community. Like Susan Sherard did at Holy Spirit in Mars Hill, North Carolina, people in your community can help visiting pilgrims find groups and experiences where they can express their gifts, longings, and passions.

♦ *Human connection around the rites.* Marriage, baptism, and burial bring people into contact with faith communities at significant moments in their life pilgrimages. Individuals and couples in a congregation can befriend these new pilgrims in the months or days before the rite and stay in contact with them long after the rite. Programs like Prepare/Enrich for marital preparation strongly recommend that churches develop teams of "mentor couples" who befriend and offer to be older companions with newlyweds during their first few years of marriage. A periodic personal card or call from the church, particularly at anniversary dates and other important seasons, connects people's individual journeys to the life of the church.

♦ *Personal thank-you contact.* If you extended the invitation, extend personal thanks, face to face. A personal note of gratitude from someone in the community echoes your personal thanks.

Multimedia Inviting

Personal invitation and follow-up are ideal. But we have many unknown neighbors in our communities. Churches can engage in various media efforts to announce events and invite people to experience their congregational life. The following are large-scale ways churches can advertise, announce, and invite.

- ♦ Mailing campaigns

- ♦ News releases and media journalist connections

- ♦ Newspaper ads

- ♦ Telephone outreach

- ♦ Email and website postings

- ♦ Low-budget or partnered radio and television spots

Congregational ministries of invitation, hospitality, and follow-up involve all members. But some members will show themselves as more invested and gifted in this evangelistic work. It will be wise for the church to invest its time and training with those who are gifted, passionate, and invested in evangelistic work, for they will lead our church's efforts at that most needed and effective grass-roots level. Congregation leaders can watch for people who have a natural affinity for evangelism or a passion to learn—and invite them personally to become involved in leading the congregation in evangelism. This is what John Cusick calls "The Jesus Method of Organizing": not seeking disciples by posting a flier or an announcement, but directly inviting people face to face.

Let us revisit the earlier restaurant exercise (on page 139). What experiences in your community of faith do you remember with delight? What is a treasure of your congregation? Is it the heartfelt worship, the conversations, the eager openness of people, the energy of young people, the healing ministry, the outreach programs? Talk with members of your faith community about how God's love is *uniquely and particularly* manifest in your midst. Just as you might describe a favorite restaurant to someone, think about how you would describe the uniqueness of your congregation.

Young people may find participating in the "come and see" part of evangelism more challenging, particularly in congregations where there are not many programs or ministries involving young people—and perhaps not many young people at all. Our local and national investment of financial, staff, and volunteer resources in ministry with young people is a direct and conspicuous form of continuing evangelism. But it will also be increasingly important for the church to train young leaders, lay and ordained, for missional work that may involve the creation of new forms of faith communities. Some of our most innovative and mission-minded young people—lay and ordained—are creating new ways of gathering, celebrating, and serving as people of faith. Older, more established congregations and ministries need to support these new "faith ventures" vigorously so that they have the best chance possible of reaching people who otherwise are not interested in darkening the door of a church. Whether these ministries take the shape of café churches, new monastic communities, social and community-building ministries, or groups committed to new faith expressions through arts and technology, they can only thrive with sufficient support and investment of trust from parents, older members, and established congregations.

Support of new ministry ventures and ministries with young people involves the following:

* *Money.* Infuse new ministries with trust by becoming investors in the new ventures. Groups of congregations, dioceses, or individuals could pool resources to create competitive annual grants given to the most promising, innovative, or strongly emerging ministries in their area.

* *Space and time.* Devote or create attractive space for the ministry or new community, and invest time in participating, helping lead, or providing institutional support.

* *Leadership training.* Young and new leaders may learn some things through the trial and error of just jumping in; but they better learn and internalize strong leadership habits through a stepwise process that introduces people to basic leadership and then expands to broader and subtler skills. Camps, extracurricular organizations, campus leadership programs, and leadership training in military, business, nursing, and community organizing settings all offer models for effective leader development.

* *Deep leadership support.* Ministries are more likely to thrive when they have an assurance of background leaders who will go to bat for them with the larger institution, run interference with institutional adversaries, and provide guidance at times of challenge. Deep leadership support involves empowering, mentoring, and getting out of the way of new leaders, while at the same time leading on other fronts and clearing institutional obstacles so that new ministries can succeed.

If we put our support fully behind new ministries, we will send a clear signal to the people that new leaders are trying to reach—that our church indeed cares about them and welcomes their companionship in our continuing journey with Christ on the way.

and now for the programmatic

I have made the case throughout this book that we need to turn toward more individual and interpersonal forms of evangelism and not rely on the institution to bear the full responsibility of proclaiming the good news. People respond to *people*. People respond to personal stories and direct expressions of wonder and joy. Without these personal connections, people may experience the church's worship as irrelevant.

But now it is time to come full circle.

The worship, programs, and gatherings of the whole congregation bring together the many disparate individual stories of God's transforming love to bear on one Great Story. In communities of disciples aware of their own gratitude, the story of God's redemptive work in Christ becomes a living story. In the journey of conversion, many people find their experiences in church—hearing a sermon, praying the Eucharistic Prayer, singing a song, watching people interact with one another, or praying or working with others—as a kind of "tipping point." Through church programs and corporate gatherings, people often come to a moment when they say, "Ah, yes, it is really true" (or, sadly, "I'm sorry, but I'm just not seeing it"). Below are some brief reminders of important evangelistic work that congregations can do.

1. WELCOMING, HOSPITALITY, AND NEW MEMBER INCORPORATION

A ministry of welcome and hospitality means attentiveness and warm receptiveness to the stranger—and a constant remembrance that we are there for others and not solely for ourselves. Programmatic solutions to the need for welcome and hospitality tend to feel programmatic, both to congregants and visitors. But if enough individuals in congregations adopt newcomer welcome as a specific way to practice their overall evangelistic spiritual discipline—"meeting my neighbor"—then welcome and hospitality become integral expressions of a congregation's spiritual life. Newcomer welcome is a perfect place to practice evangelistic listening and naming the Holy. As individuals engage in "meeting their neighbors" at church, conversations lead to people sharing their interests and affinities with each other, and it becomes easy for newcomers to find people with whom they can explore their own sense of meaning and contribution.

When meeting someone, it is not necessary to ask if he is new to the church. You can simply begin conversation, asking him about life and talking about your own life. Some churches have adopted this strategy by printing "coffee-hour topics" in each week's bulletin. Suggestions of affinity topics for conversation help people connect to one another in new ways—long-term members and newcomers alike. This levels the playing field and takes the pressure off welcoming by simply drawing people into conversations with each other: "How many siblings did you have in your family?" "What were your most memorable holiday traditions?" Congregations will become livelier simply by fostering these kinds of conversations between people, as members and newcomers alike make new discoveries.

2. PREACHING, TEACHING, AND SMALL GROUP ENCOUNTER

At the heart of Christian proclamation, instruction, and fellowship is our hope that we and others will witness, recognize, name, and celebrate the Holy in our lives. Sermons, classes, and groups give people ways of interpreting, reframing, and redirecting their own thoughts and motivations. It is time to begin a shift toward a more evangelistic focus in the pulpit. Most fundamentally, this involves expecting people to show up who do not yet know God's love or the basic stories.

An evangelistic focus in preaching involves:

1) unapologetically speaking truth in love;

2) giving up the assumption that we are preaching to an in-crowd, instead committing to clarity by explaining up-front our hidden or over-rehearsed Episcopal scripts;

3) helping people see and rediscover their encounter with the living Christ;

4) including newcomers and strangers by acknowledging their perspectives;

5) demonstrating that it is possible to name the Holy, in our own lives as well as the lives of others, and daring to offer our own witness to the wonder and fallibility of being human and to God's grace in all of that humanness.

Teaching events are most effective when they include time for small group discussions in which people can interact with themes by speaking from their own experiences. Programs for Christian instruction and formation include Alpha and Via Media, designed as evangelistic instruction and discussion programs to which individuals can invite interested friends and colleagues; Disciples of Christ in Community (DOCC), a twenty-week immersion in Christian beliefs and practices that includes weekly instruction and small group discussion; Cursillo, an intensive weekend immersion in Christianity that involves instruction, small group discussion, and worship; and Faith Alive, a weekend focused on Christian renewal and commitment. All of these, along with other evangelistic teaching events like Theology on Tap, provide opportunities for individuals to invite their friends, neighbors, or colleagues with whom they have already shared their stories of wonder and gratitude to "come and see" more about our Christian faith. Small groups vary in purpose and duration, but recent small group models have stressed the importance of a group covenant having purpose, duration, open membership, and a pattern of prayerful self-disclosure and shared *midrash* on each other's lives as places of the Holy.

3. SERVICE: THE ACTION-REFLECTION MODEL
Only some people will be drawn to faith or hear God's invitation to new life in sermons or the rites of the church. Many youth and young adults are more drawn to communities and groups where they feel they can make a difference in the world. Groups like the Interfaith Youth Core in Chicago, Illinois, the youth group in Winslow and Holbrook, Arizona, and the faith-and-business meetings in Mountain View, California, bring social action and deep spiritual reflection together. It is powerful for volunteers to meet together and share their experiences with each other and with a broader group of people. It is also powerful for people serving and served to come together to reflect on their experiences of grace with one another.

The action-reflection approach can be part of our unique offering to any public work in which we participate. This action-reflection process can add a new and rich dimension to the "deeds-based evangelism" for which our church is known. As much as possible, our service ministries should be publicly advertised, open to public participation, and in cooperation with other churches, businesses, and religious and social organizations.

4. WORSHIP AND MUSIC

Worship tends to be one of the "hot buttons" in any discussion of evangelism, renewal, or church growth. People have clear ideas, whether right or wrong in a given context, about what is most inviting or evangelistic—which may have more to do with their own attachments and revulsions than with a primary focus on offering God's good news in the clearest, most evocative way.

At the end of the day, it is not clear that one form of worship or one style of music is superior as an evangelistic witness. Ancient or modern, plebian or proletariat, strictly by-the-book or wildly novel—it is possible for any form or style to be delivered well or poorly. I have served six different congregations as an organist, choir director, and music ensemble leader, as well as a priest, and I have helped direct liturgical planning in three different congregations. I have seen problems and blessings with all forms.

People make basic judgments about worship when they come to a church: Is there *passion* and is there *quality*? In other words, do people seem to believe what they are doing or saying? Do congregation members seem engaged or bored? Is the liturgy smooth and natural, clear of haphazard uncertainties? Does the worship clearly communicate the gospel from beginning to end? Is music performed and led well, and does it draw people into deeper prayer and worship?

Most essentially, when planning and evaluating worship, teams should ask, "Is our worship getting across with any power to the stranger in our midst?" This kind of question challenges us to consider ways to introduce moments of surprise or startling clarity into our liturgies and music—which can become reawakening moments for all the faithful.

5. SACRAMENTAL LIFE TRANSITIONS

People come or return to churches at significant moments of transition in their lives and the lives of their families. We mark some of these moments particularly in weddings, baptisms, and funerals. For weddings, many churches require the couple to worship regularly and get involved in classes and events. Most clergy require a series of premarital counseling sessions, although these vary widely in quality and focus. But only a small percentage of churches take advantage of a model suggested by Prepare/Enrich, where an engaged couple is paired with a mentor couple in the congregation for more intensive fellowship and conversation about married life. More importantly, there is opportunity for follow-up with a couple after the wedding, through personal check-ins, invitations by individuals and groups to gatherings, and cards at anniversaries.

Heather and I went through an intensive birthing class before the birth of our first daughter. As we watched rather remarkable videos and talked about very intimate details of the birth process, we formed a kind of community with people in the class. Every class concluded with a "spiritual moment" of passing a candle around and saying what in the class was important that week. Heather and I found ourselves wondering why churches didn't have these kinds of classes, where the sense of community could continue beyond the end of the course and beyond birth. Faith Inkubators provides some rich material for parents from birth through baptism through school to graduation, and the program brings parents together at regular intervals to help them learn about continuing faith formation with their children in the home. But a powerful extension of this would be churches offering birth classes, and young parents being paired with another mentoring family and "surrogate grandparents."

With funerals, there are many missed opportunities for follow-up with family members and friends—and this cannot be the sole work of ordained ministers and church staff, nor can it fall on a few volunteers. When my mother died, members from the Evangelical Mennonite congregation we had joined came in a steady stream for weeks with food and friendship. I remember being so grateful for that outpouring of love and care—and also wishing later that people would have continued to check in with us, as it took me over a year to awaken fully to my grief. Churches can learn from hospice organizations about the best ways to be with people in grief, over months and years of bereavement.

In all these moments of sacramental life transition, evangelism is a continuing ministry of bearing good news to others through our gifts of presence and friendship, sharing our stories, and walking holy ground with people who may not yet know how profoundly holy it is.

---

new ways of thinking

As a final note, there are some movements in the church that challenge us to think in new ways about evangelism. They include seeker services, house church, the Emerging Church movement, New Monasticism, and church planting, as well as web-based communities and evangelistic efforts. It would be easy to commit an entire chapter or book to each of these movements, in which committed clergy and lay leaders work together to create new approaches to corporate worship and expression of Christian faith—with the central aim of freeing God's good news from clichés and tired routines so that it may be heard afresh by people who do not yet know how much God loves them.

Some may wish to dismiss these efforts as simplistic, market-driven, over-enthusiastic, or spiritually shallow. But behind these very different methods and approaches lies one common commitment—making the saving and ennobling work of Jesus Christ known to people who would not usually choose to darken the door of a typical institutionally habitualized church. The Church of England is beginning to embrace partnership with these movements and efforts across the United Kingdom, allowing the church to have a much more fluid life with many new expressions such as alt.worship, Base Ecclesial Communities, café churches, cell churches, midweek congregations, community-organizing faith communities, seeker churches, and youth and young adult congregations.[23]

> When I went to our bishop with the idea of COTA, he gave his blessing and support, as long as I accepted episcopal oversight. I said, "Okay, bishop. But no leashes." At first, he didn't know what to make of that. "What?" But then, he said, "Okay. Okay, Karen, no leashes." — *Karen Ward, abbess of the joint Lutheran-Episcopal congregation and new monastic community Church of the Apostles (COTA)*

There is a concept at play in these approaches that can be a bit unnerving to our institutional structures and attachments: "Unleashed ministry." These new types of communities—as well as many of the communities of faith described in this book—practice a kind of "unleashed ministry," where lay people and clergy alike are set free to develop and pursue ministries of their choosing, both inside and outside the church. Such freedom generates excitement, sparks imagination, and encourages a spiritually enriching examination of assumptions. All this leads to communities of people offering a powerful witness to the profligate, effervescent generosity of God through the Body of Christ.

SEEKER SERVICE

Rick Warren, in his definition of a seeker service, may offer the best summary of contemporary efforts. He has identified three "nonnegotiable elements of a seeker service: 1) treat unbelievers with love and respect; 2) relate the service to their needs; and 3) share the message in a practical, understandable manner. All other elements," Rick concludes, "are secondary issues that churches shouldn't get hung up on."

The focus on "keeping it real" in these new church gatherings means that the conversations and worship expressions may seem a bit gritty, as sacred and profane meet in sometimes surprising ways. But Rick Warren also offers an important observation—one that returns us to the emphasis of this book. "A service geared toward seekers is meant to supplement personal evangelism, not replace it. People generally find it easier to decide for Christ when there are multiple relationships supporting that decision."[24] In other words, evangelism depends most fundamentally on us as individual Christians living out our Baptismal Covenant to proclaim God's good news by word and example and to find and love Christ in each person. How much we are willing to embrace these elements of our Baptismal Covenant as our core spiritual passions will free our hearts and minds to be as creative, resourceful, and attentive as we can, so that we may follow wherever the Holy Spirit may lead us.

"Were Not Our Hearts Burning Within Us?"

Then their eyes were opened, and they recognized him; and he vanished from their sight. They said to each other, "Were not our hearts burning within us?" (Luke 24:31–32)

Two disciples, wandering the roads outside the city, share with one another their grief and confusion as they tried to make sense of the journey they had been on with Jesus—a journey that had ended so abruptly and violently. Two disciples, uncertain of the future, review the events that had changed their lives and left them as perpetual pilgrims—unable to return to life as they knew it with Jesus, and with no clear sense of what was ahead.

Two disciples are joined by a stranger who keeps apace with them and listens to their conversation. He asks a question. They tell their story. And he names for them the Holy that they were unable to see. Now the two have become three, as the disciples listen with increasing hope and joy to the stranger who has become their guide. Responding to the stirring of their hearts, they beg their companion to stay with them. And then, around a table in a place that is none of their homes, the stranger who is now a friend blesses their common bread and divides it for them to share. Wonder fills the room. Easter dawns in that moment, as two wandering disciples recognize for the first time the one who is with them.

And then the moment is over. But wonder and gratitude remain. Impelled by the force of their awakening, they take to the road again immediately, rushing by night to find their friends back in the city to tell them their amazing good news. As they tell one disciple after another, again the world changes, expanding before them as they share their stories of meeting the Christ.

At the end of the day, evangelism as a spiritual practice is most basically about waking up. It means rousing from slumber and paying attention to life—all of life—with all our senses attuned and our minds and hearts ready to respond, as daily we encounter God's loving work in us and the entire world.

But we alone cannot rouse ourselves from slumber. It is so easy for us to become self-absorbed, as individuals and as a church. John Wesley was right: We need some manner of awakening like the disciples experienced on the way to Emmaus—God again and again opening our eyes. But we can keep ourselves ready by living fully attuned to ourselves, others, and the world around us, bearing in our hearts and minds and voices the stories of our journeys, and praying with expectant desire that we will see the One who is waiting to meet us. When we are stirred to life, and when we tell the stories of God's gifts in our lives to others, we will hear stories of wonder and joy in return, and wonder will beget wonder, joy beget joy. Each moment of transformation *is* the eschaton begun, and we are beckoned on a journey that takes us all, as C. S. Lewis put it, "further up and further in."

Living the Christian life—the evangelistic life—is living in pilgrimage. It means leaving the psychological comfort of our homes (including our parish refuges), free of props, in the companionship of fellow pilgrims, as we seek and speak the presence of the Holy. We are propelled out beyond our reveries and self-preoccupations to meet Christ on the road. And that is where we find the church, born again in new places among new people by the power of the Holy Spirit.

In my late twenties, after I had failed and left my first marriage, after a year of wandering in my own anger, shame, and confusion, I found myself seeking to confess. I met with a Jesuit priest, and poured out my story. I knelt, and he placed his hands on my head and said, "God has removed all your sin." I remember being overtaken by an image in my mind of Christ's hands holding the world, just as this priest held my head in his hands, and seeing a glimpse of how vast and complete God's grace was for the whole world—and for me. I was taken in gratitude and wonder beyond my self-preoccupation and began my pilgrimage anew.

Getting evangelism right is living your Christian life, bumps and all, and ready to tell your stories and name God's work for what it is. Getting evangelism right will not mean reaching the promised land or finding perfection in this life, either as individuals or as communities of faith. Getting evangelism right means living as a pilgrim, following after wonder and delight, and being prepared to share from the treasure-house of your life the great unfolding story of God's redeeming work.

Episcopalians are indeed part of a small denomination. In the United States alone, among over 300 million people, with our membership less than one percent of the population, and our weekly attendance less than one million, we cannot pretend that we are a shiny city set on a hill. But we can be something much more powerful. We can be the leaven in the dough—a lively and life-giving influence in all the communities around us. We already are doing this to some extent in our social ministry. But we also have the opportunity to spread like leaven in the dough of our society and transform the very nature of public discourse and consciousness. People might begin again to speak of God and to discuss their spiritual lives with freedom in public places. By our presence in various groups and meetings, by our gentle new habit of speaking, others may become more conscious of the invitation to new life God has put before them, and bring it with them into their families, bars, clubs, blogs, and boardrooms.

If we get this kind of evangelism right—at all levels of our church, from the young to the old, from new convert to lifelong member, from layperson to bishop, across all groups of people—then the life of the church will begin to look very different indeed. What if bishops dedicated five hours each week to leaving their offices and going out to engage in evangelistic listening with neighbors and strangers in their communities? What if our bishops and the rectors of our largest parishes scheduled for themselves at least one circuit-riding tour of evangelistic conversations and public preaching every year, making connections in places that take them away from the ecclesiastical business that can otherwise absorb all their attention? What if our deacons helped train people in the practice of evangelism, helping us all learn to become comfortable in our Christian skin and living as public followers of Jesus?

But no efforts of ordained leaders will have true and lasting effect if we as the entire pilgrim people of God abdicate our responsibility to listen for and speak good news wherever we are. Without transforming our own discourse with one another and our daily habits of adoration and gratitude, all the efforts of church leaders will once again return to a top-down attempt at recruiting people to join a club devoted to itself.

Evangelism is every Christian's response to God. It does not require verbal gymnastics, flawless theological knowledge, great acts of philanthropy, or seamless strategies for incorporating new members. It requires you to tell your story. It requires you to listen to others, attentive to signs of God's presence. It requires you to live fully, be fully awake, and stir others to wakefulness. If some critical mass (say, ten thousand of us) do this faithfully, we will be yeast scattered through our communities, raising people's minds and hearts to God. This will transform the world around us—and this will transform the church. We will be that community of pilgrims, sinners redeemed, lovers of God, who come together from time to time in our ongoing journeys to remind ourselves of the stories of grace that propel us ever onward.

More elementally, we ourselves will be transformed. When I first started teaching psychology, I had already completed an intensive two-year master's program in which I read more than I had ever read before. For two years I soaked in knowledge like a sponge—willingly or unwillingly! But it was not until I taught courses in psychology to undergraduates that I really internalized and owned my knowledge of psychology. I didn't really "know" psychology until I taught it. It is the same with our embracing ministry and evangelism. It is only by *practice* that we know—and will continue to know—our faith more fully. Our stories take root more firmly and have greater impact on us when we share them publicly with others. Furthermore, our understanding of Christ grows as we meet others and hear their stories and share their bread. Then we will find ourselves reflecting in new ways on our sense of pilgrimage: "Where am I being sent now?"

There is no perfect way of sharing our faith with others. But the more we are awake and alert, the more we become attuned to the questions that people will bring to us along the way; the more we listen closely and deeply, the more we learn to respond. When our daughter Cassie was two years old, she once told us at bedtime prayers,

"No, Jesus doesn't love me!" After getting over my initial shock, I asked her, "Why?" She could not tell me. Later, when we told her that her new baby sister, Miriam, loved her, she said, "No, Miriam doesn't love me!" When I asked, "Why?" she said, "Miriam can't hold me"—which is true for a new baby. Then something dawned on me and I asked her, "Is that why you think Jesus doesn't love you?" She said, "Yeah. Jesus can't hold me." And so we opened a new chapter in our sharing stories with her about Jesus, and about what it means to love and be loved.

When rightly engaged, evangelism *is* worship. Sound evangelism leads us to recognizing the Holy Spirit and adoring the Christ. Can you imagine any number of us engaging in this profound act of worship in our day-to-day lives? In communities of faith where naming the Holy becomes a natural part of life, worship becomes a culmination and indeed a true icon of people's lives in Christ. In such transformed communities, our church will celebrate the Holy Spirit, speak openly of Jesus, and name the Holy without shame or anxiety. Our church will truly be a house for all people. Until our final transformation at the end of ages, that will be about as close as we can hope to come to the kingdom of God.

There are many elements of evangelism I have not explored in this book. That is because I wanted to focus on what is most fundamental, on what helps support any evangelistic work in social ministry, church growth, worship, and public advocacy. Speaking our own stories and hearing others' is the first and most basic element of the spiritual practice of evangelism—and if we really embrace the fundamentals, all the rest will follow.

A Guide for Discussion

You may of course read the books in this series on your own, but because they focus on the transformation of the Episcopal Church in the twenty-first century the books are especially useful as a basis for discussion and reflection within a congregation or community. The questions below are intended to generate fruitful discussion about how members of the group have experienced and practiced evangelism not only within the institutional church, but also more broadly in all aspects of their lives. The questions therefore focus both on what has been helpful and what has been lacking; on how the church has been supportive and where it has fallen short.

Each group will identify its own needs and will be shaped by the interests of the participants and their comfort in sharing personal life stories. Discussion leaders will wish to focus on particular areas that address the concerns and goals of the group, using the questions and themes provided here simply as suggestions for a place to start the conversation.

chapter one

"Go Therefore and Make Disciples"

Gortner opens this chapter with his definition of evangelism as a spiritual practice: "Evangelism is your natural expression of gratitude for God's goodness." He goes on to note that "true evangelism emerges only out of your own transformation" (pp. 1–2).

- How would you define "evangelism"? What associations or images come to mind when you hear the word "evangelism"?

- Do you see evangelism as a spiritual practice, or something else? How do you practice evangelism in your own life? What are your "habits of evangelism"?

- What has been your experience or impression of the evangelistic efforts made by the religious communities you have known? Who have been the evangelists in your life?

♦ ♦ ♦ ♦ ♦

On page 29 Gortner offers a list of eight "core assertions" for evangelism in a new century. Read these statements aloud, and reflect on their implications by asking the following questions of each.

- What do you make of this assertion? Does it ring true to your experience of and hope for the church in the twenty-first century?

- What in this assertion affirms the way you practice evangelism in your congregation?

- What in this assertion challenges the way you practice evangelism in your congregation?

chapter two

"The Road to Jerusalem is in the Heart"

In this chapter Gortner describes the need for seeing our Christian lives as pilgrimage in order to name "the presence of the Holy" in the lives of people we encounter (p. 34). Although each of our stories of pilgrimage is unique, there are common themes "of seeking and uncertainty, finding and being found, relief from burdens too heavy to bear, the gratification of discovering Love, and deep, transformative gratitude and wonder" (p. 36–37).

+ How would you describe your spiritual journey? Where did your pilgrimage begin? Where has it taken you?

+ Which of the "common themes" Gortner identifies do you recognize in your life?

+ What other themes do you hear in the stories of Christian pilgrimage shared in your discussion, or in your reading or listening to others?

+   +   +   +   +

Gortner states: "All mission—and, as a consequence, all evangelism—begins, proceeds, and ends with the Holy Spirit" (p. 40).

+ How would this understanding of the role of the Holy Spirit change the way your congregation practices mission and evangelism?

+ When have you experienced the "fruits of the Spirit" (p. 43) and recognized them as such? What or who helped you see them as signs of God's active presence in your life? Did you tell anyone about this experience?

chapter three

Living the Pilgrim Faith

Gortner describes this chapter as a "travel guide" to a number of places where intentionally evangelistic ministries are flourishing and "seeds of transformation are being sown" (p. 70). He focuses on how evangelism is uniquely expressed in each place, and includes interviews with members as well as some history of how the focus on evangelism came to be central to the ministry.

- What stood out for you in the stories of these communities?

- If your congregation were to be included in this "travel guide," how would you describe its history in terms of ministries of evangelism? Who would you need to interview—from the past or the present—in order to tell its story?

- What ministries or events or decisions taken by the congregation would you highlight?

◆　◆　◆　◆　◆

Gortner also describes several programs that have been developed for parish-based evangelism and faith renewal, such as Alpha and Cursillo (p. 108).

- What experience do you have of these or other parish-based programs for evangelism and renewal?

- In your experience, how effective are such programs in sowing the "seeds of transformation"? What makes them effective?

- What can hinder the ability of these programs to create a community of believers who embrace the telling of their stories as a spiritual discipline?

chapter four

With Open and Courageous Hearts

Gortner identifies in this chapter several "habits for evangelism": practicing gratitude, learning to listen, and naming the holy.

* How have you practiced these habits in your life?

* In what ways do you experience these habits being practiced in your congregation?

* What or who encourages the development of these habits in your life? In your congregation? Who or what discourages them?

◆ ◆ ◆ ◆ ◆

Turn to the exercise "Where is God Here?" on page 147.

* How could you adapt this exercise to the needs and circumstances of your discussion group?

* Develop a plan on how you will practice this exercise now or in the coming week—how you will divide into pairs or small groups, where you will go, to whom you will talk, what you will ask, and when you will return to report your findings.

* What are your hopes and expectations, your misgivings and concerns, as you envision doing this exercise?

"Were Not Our Hearts Burning Within Us?"

In this chapter Gortner states: "Getting evangelism right means living as a pilgrim, following after wonder and delight, and being prepared to share from the treasure-house of your life the great unfolding story of God's redeeming work" (p. 167).

- ✦ What do you need to sustain your life as a pilgrim?

- ✦ What do you need to be better prepared to share the "story of God's redeeming work" in your life?

- ✦ What is stopping you from telling your story?

✦ ✦ ✦ ✦ ✦

Gortner speculates that if we "get this kind of evangelism right" then "the life of the church will begin to look very different indeed" (p. 168).

- ✦ What do you imagine the Episcopal Church would look like if more of its members saw themselves as practicing evangelists?

- ✦ How would the Episcopal Church look different if its ordained leaders placed evangelism as their top priority? What aspects of church life would change? How would their ministries be different?

- ✦ How can we reset our priorities? How can we move around, over, under, or through what stands in our way in order to encourage renewal throughout church?

Resources

recommended books on evangelism

Bass, Diana Butler and Joseph Stewart-Sicking. *From Nomads to Pilgrims: Stories from Practicing Congregations.* Herndon, Va.: Alban Institute, 2006.

Bass, Dorothy, ed. *Practicing Our Faith.* San Francisco: Jossey-Bass, 1997.

Beaudoin, Tom. *Virtual Faith: The Irreverent Spiritual Quest of Generation X.* San Francisco: Jossey-Bass, 1998.

Chandler, Russell. *Feeding the Flock: Restaurants and Churches You'd Stand in Line For.* Herndon, Va.: The Alban Institute, 1998.

Eck, Diana. *Encountering God: A Spiritual Journey from Bozeman to Banaras.* Boston: Beacon Press, 1993.

McLaren, Brian. *A New Kind of Christian: A Tale of Two Friends on a Spiritual Journey.* San Francisco: Jossey-Bass, 2001.

Schmitt, Jacqueline, and David Gortner, "The Episcopal Church Welcomes You? Evangelizing Students and Young

Adults," in Sheryl Kujawa, ed., *Disorganized Religion: The Evangelization of Youth and Young Adults*. Cambridge, Mass.: Cowley Publications, 1998.

Tomlin, Graham. *The Provocative Church*. London: Society for Promoting Christian Knowledge, 2002.

Webber, Robert. *Ancient-Future Evangelism*. Grand Rapids: Baker, 2003.

Notes
and Sources

notes

1. *The Influence of the Church on Modern Problems: Papers by Various Writers Read at the Church Congress in 1922* (New York: Macmillan, 1922); Wade Clark Roof, Bruce Greer, Mary Johnson, and Andrea Leibson, *Generation of Seekers: The Spiritual Journeys of the Baby Boom Generation* (San Francisco: HarperSanFrancisco, 1994).
2. Kirk Hadaway, *A Report on Episcopal Churches in the United States* (New York: The Domestic and Foreign Missionary Society PECUSA, 2002). Dale E. Jones, Sherri Doty, Clifford Grammich, and James E. Horsch, *Religious Congregations & Membership in the United States 2000: An Enumeration by Region, State and County Based on Data Reported for 149 Religious Bodies* (Cincinnati: Glenmary Research Center, 2002). Valparaiso University's geography department has posted from the Glenmary research a series of very helpful maps showing county by county the density of religious affiliation of various denominations in the United States, at www.valpo.edu/geomet/geo/courses/geo200/religion.html.
3. Kit and Frederica Konolige, *The Power of Their Glory: America's Ruling Class: The Episcopalians* (New York: Wyden, 1978). Emile Durkheim, *The Elementary Forms of the Religious Life,* trans. J. W. Swain (Glencoe, Ill.: Free Press, 1954).

4. David Gortner and John Dreibelbis, "Mentoring Clergy for Effective Leadership," in *Reflective Practice: Supervision and Formation in Ministry* 27 (2007): 62–82; John Dreibelbis and David Gortner, "Beyond Wish-lists for Pastoral Leadership: Assessing Clergy Behavior and Congregational Outcomes to Guide Seminary Curriculum," in *Theological Education* 40 (2005): 25–49.

5. Phil Schwadel and Christian Smith, *Portraits of Protestant Teens: A Report on Teenagers in Major U.S. Denominations* (Chapel Hill: National Study of Youth and Religion, 2005); results presented have been collated from summary tables.

6. William S. Korn and Giles L. Asbury, "Where Have All the Young Ones Gone . . ." *Plumbline* (Summer 2000): 16–20. Korn and Asbury review the 1993 CIRP Freshman Survey results for Episcopalians: "A high percentage of our young people has decided to change their religious affiliation before they even have a chance to meet their local chaplain."

7. Julius A. Schaad, *Evangelism in the Church: An Appeal to Christians* (New York, 1927). Cited and summarized on the Episcopal Church website, under "Office for Liturgy and Music: Bishops' Crusade."

8. *The Lambeth Conference 1948: The Encyclical Letter from the Bishops; together with Resolutions and Reports* (London: SPCK, 1948), resolution 37, p. 35.

9. Michael Green, *Evangelism in the Early Church,* revised edition (Eastbourne: Kingsway Communications, 2003), 12.

10. Donald McGavran, *Understanding Church Growth,* third edition (Grand Rapids: Eerdmans, 1990), 146.

11. George Hunter III, *How to Reach Secular People* (Nashville: Abingdon Press, 1992), 83–85.

12. Carol Lytch, *Choosing Church* (Louisville: Westminster John Knox Press), 2003.

13. M. O'Keefe, "'None' Becoming Religion of Choice for Many in U.S.," *Chicago Tribune* (December 5, 2003).

14. Martin Robinson, "Pilgrimage and Mission," in C. Bartholomew and F. Hughes, eds., *Explorations in a Christian Theology of Pilgrimage* (Burlington, Vt.: Ashgate, 2004), 178.

15. J. Moltmann, *The Source of Life: The Holy Spirit and the Theology of Life* (Minneapolis: Fortress, 1997), 5.

16. David Bosch, *Transforming Mission* (Maryknoll, N.Y.: Orbis Books, 1991), 415.

17. Green, *Evangelism in the Early Church,* 17–24.

18. K. H. Ting, *Love Never Ends* (Nanjing, China: Yilin Press, 2000), 142, 149. For a fuller discussion, see Tobias Brandner, "K. H. Ting's Theological Motifs in *Love Never Ends,*" in *Seeking Truth in Love,* ed.

Wang Peng (Hong Kong: Amity Press, 2006), 209.

19. From K. H. Ting, "My View of God," quoted in Donald Messer, "The Chinese Banyan Tree Theology of Bishop K. H. Ting," in *Seeking Truth in Love,* 282.

20. Quoted in Raymond Whitehead, "The Life and Work of a Chinese Christian," in *No Longer Strangers,* ed. Raymond Whitehead (Maryknoll, N.Y.: Orbis Books, 1989), 18.

21. "BLSN Infuses Business Leaders with Spirituality" by Joan Passarelli, *Los Altos Town Crier* (December 12, 2001).

22. John Cusick and Katherine DeVries, *The Basic Guide to Young Adult Ministry* (Maryknoll, N.Y.: Orbis Books, 2001).

23. *Mission-Shaped Church: Church Planting and Fresh Expressions of Church in a Changing Context* (London: Church House Publishing, 2004), 44.

24. Rick Warren, *The Purpose-Driven Church: Growth without Compromising Mission* (Grand Rapids: Zondervan, 1992), 246–247.

———

sources quoted

Quotations set apart within the chapters have been taken from the following books and articles.

Marc Andrus, quoted in the *San Francisco Chronicle* online, Matthai Chakko Kuruvila, "New Bishop has Broad Diocese: Mark [sic] Andrus to Lead Bay Area's Episcopal Church" (July 21, 2006).

David Bosch, *Transforming Mission* (Maryknoll, N.Y.: Orbis Books, 1991), 413.

Kenda Creasy Dean, *Practicing Passion: Youth and the Quest for a Passionate Church* (Grand Rapids: Zondervan, 2006), 108.

Charles Fulton and Jim Lemler, *Truth and Hope: A Time of Truth and Hope in the Episcopal Church* (Cincinnati: Forward Movement Publications), 2006.

Brother John of Taizé, "The Pilgrimage Seen through the Bible," *Lumen Vitae* 39:1 (1984): 393.

Michael Green, *Evangelism in the Early Church,* revised edition (Eastbourne: Kingsway Communications, 2003), 13, 24.

Richard Gula, *Reason Informed by Faith: Foundations of Catholic Morality* (Mahwah, N.J.: Paulist Press, 1989), 52.

William McKinney, quoted in Warren Goldstein, "The New Evangelists: Yale Divinity School and the Revival of the Christian Left," *Yale Alumni Magazine* (November/December 2006).

Jürgen Moltmann, *The Spirit of Life: A Universal Affirmation* (Minneapolis: Augsburg Fortress, 1992), 98.

Cyril Okorocha, "Evangelism in the Anglican Communion: An Overview," in *Anglicanism: A Global Communion* (New York: Church Publishing, 1998), 328.

Geoff Pearson, *Toward the Conversion of England,* Grove Evangelism Series #7 (Cambridge: Grove Books, 2005), 14.

Lewis Rambo, "The Psychology of Religious Conversion," presented at the International Coalition for Religious Freedom Conference, Berlin, Germany (May 29–31, 1998).

Martin Robinson, "Pilgrimage and Mission," in C. Bartholomew and F. Hughes, eds., *Explorations in a Christian Theology of Pilgrimage* (Burlington, Vt.: Ashgate, 2004), 177.

W. Taylor Stevenson, *Anglican Theological Review,* special supplementary collection of papers on evangelism (1979), vi.

K. H. Ting, *Love Never Ends* (Nanjing, China: Yilin Press, 2000), 418.

K. H. Ting, *God is Love* (Colorado Springs: Cook Communications Ministries International, 2004), 315.